THE POWER OF
I AM

TWO WORDS THAT WILL CHANGE
YOUR LIFE TODAY

JOEL OSTEEN

New York   Boston   Nashville

ALSO BY JOEL OSTEEN

Break Out!

Break Out! Journal

Daily Readings from Break Out!

Every Day a Friday

Every Day a Friday Journal

Daily Readings from Every Day a Friday

I Declare

I Declare Personal Application Guide

You Can, You Will

You Can, You Will Journal

Daily Readings from You Can, You Will

Your Best Life Now

Daily Readings from Your Best Life Now

Your Best Life Begins Each Morning

Your Best Life Now Study Guide

Your Best Life Now for Moms

Your Best Life Now Journal

Starting Your Best Life Now

THE POWER OF
I AM

One Scripture is noted from *The Message*. Copyright © 1993, 1994, 1995, 1996, 2000, 2001, 2002. Used by permission of NavPress Publishing Group.

Literary development: Koechel,Peterson & Associates, Inc., Minneapolis, Minnesota.

FaithWords
Hachette Book Group
1290 Avenue of the Americas
New York, NY 10104

www.faithwords.com

Printed in the United States of America

RRD-H

First Edition: October 2015
10   9   8   7   6   5   4   3   2   1

FaithWords is a division of Hachette Book Group, Inc. The FaithWords name and logo are trademarks of Hachette Book Group, Inc.

The Hachette Speakers Bureau provides a wide range of authors for speaking events. To find out more, go to www.hachettespeakersbureau.com or call (866) 376-6591.

The publisher is not responsible for websites (or their content) that are not owned by the publisher.

Library of Congress Cataloging-in-Publication Data

Osteen, Joel.
    The power of I am : two words that will change your life today / Joel Osteen.—First Edition.
        pages cm
    ISBN 978-0-89296-996-8 (hardcover)—ISBN 978-1-4555-3620-7 (hardcover large print)—ISBN 978-1-60941-904-2 (audio cd)—ISBN 978-1-4789-0519-6 (audio download)—ISBN 978-1-4789-0828-9 (audio playway)—ISBN 978-0-89296-997-5 (ebook)   I. Self-confidence—Religious aspects—Christianity.   2. Affirmations.
3. Self-talk—Religious aspects—Christianity.   I. Title.
    BV4598.23.O88 2015
    248.4—dc23
                                                                          2015025973

ISBN 978-1-4555-6387-6 (international ed.); ISBN 978-1-4555-6514-6 (autographed ed.); ISBN 978-1-4555-3857-7 (B&N autographed ed.); ISBN 978-1-60941-832-8 (Spanish ed.); ISBN 978-1-4555-3808-9 (Spanish ebook ed.)

This book is dedicated to my wife, Victoria, who inspires me and fills my life with love and light, and to my children, Jonathan and Alexandra, who continue to amaze me and fill my life with joy. I am grateful to God for bringing us together as a family and for showing me that I am blessed.

ACKNOWLEDGMENTS

In this book I offer many stories shared with me by friends, members of our congregation, and people I've met around the world. I appreciate and acknowledge their contributions and support. Some of those mentioned in the book are people I have not met personally, and, in a few cases, we've changed the names to protect the privacy of individuals. I give honor to all those to whom honor is due. As the son of a church leader and a pastor myself, I've listened to countless sermons and presentations, so in some cases I can't remember the exact source of a story.

I am indebted to the amazing staff of Lakewood Church, the wonderful members of Lakewood who share their stories with me, and those around the world who generously support our ministry and make it possible to bring hope to a world in need. I am grateful to all of those who follow our services on television, the Internet, and through the podcasts. You are all part of our Lakewood family.

I offer special thanks also to all the pastors across the country who are members of our Champions Network.

Once again, I am grateful for a wonderful team of professionals who helped me put this book together for you. Leading them is my FaithWords/Hachette publisher, Rolf Zettersten, along with team members Patsy Jones, Billy Clark, Becky Hughes, and Megan

Gerrity. I truly appreciate the editorial contributions of wordsmith Lance Wubbels.

I am grateful also to my literary agents Jan Miller Rich and Shannon Marven at Dupree Miller & Associates.

And last but not least, thanks to my wife, Victoria, and our children, Jonathan and Alexandra, who are my sources of daily inspiration, as well as to our closest family members who serve as day-to-day leaders of our ministry, including my brother, Paul, and his wife, Jennifer; my sister Lisa and her husband, Kevin; and my brother-in-law Don and his wife, Jackelyn.

CONTENTS

THE POWER OF
I AM

CHAPTER ONE

The Power of "I Am"

Lacy was a beautiful young lady who seemed to have everything going for her. She was smart, attractive, and came from a loving family. As we visited in the lobby after a service, she was friendly and had a pleasant personality. I thought if anybody would be happy, it would be her. But I soon realized it was just the opposite of what I thought. Lacy began to describe how she wasn't fulfilled; she was lonely and she perceived her coworkers as more talented. She made statements such as, "I am unattractive. I am unlucky. I am a slow learner. I am always tired."

After five minutes of listening to Lacy, I knew exactly what was holding her back. Her "I am"s. What follows those two simple words will determine what kind of life you live. "I am blessed. I am strong. I am healthy." Or, "I am slow. I am unattractive. I am a lousy mother." The "I am"s coming out of your mouth will bring either success or failure.

All through the day the power of "I am" is at work. We make a mistake and out of our mouth tumbles, "I am so clumsy." We look in the mirror, shake our head, and say, "I am so old." We see somebody who we think is more talented and whisper under our breath,

"I am so average." We get caught in traffic and grump, "I am so unlucky." Many times we wield the power of "I am" against ourselves. We don't realize how it's affecting our future.

> *Whatever follows the "I am" will eventually find you.*

Here's the principle. *Whatever follows the "I am" will eventually find you.*

When you say, "I am so clumsy," clumsiness comes looking for you. "I am so old." Wrinkles come looking for you. "I am so overweight." Calories come looking for you. It's as though you're inviting them. Whatever you follow the "I am" with, you're handing it an invitation, opening the door, and giving it permission to be in your life.

The good news is you get to choose what follows the "I am." When you go through the day saying, "I am blessed," blessings come looking for you. "I am talented." Tal-

> *The good news is you get to choose what follows the "I am."*

ent comes looking for you. You may not feel up to par, but when you say, "I am healthy," health starts heading your way. "I am strong." Strength starts tracking you down. You're inviting those things into your life.

That's why you have to be careful what follows the "I am." Don't ever say, "I am so unlucky. I never get any good breaks." You're inviting disappointments. "I am so broke. I am so in debt." You are inviting struggle. You're inviting lack.

You need to send out some new invitations. Get up in the morning and invite good things into your life. "I am blessed. I am strong. I am talented. I am wise. I am disciplined. I am focused. I am prosperous." When you talk like that, talent gets summoned by Almighty God: "Go find that person." Health, strength, abundance, and discipline start heading your way.

But how many of us, when we get up in the morning, look in the mirror and the first thing we say is, "I am so old. I am so wrinkled. I am so worn out." You are inviting oldness. You're inviting fatigue. Do us all a favor; stop inviting that. Dare to say, "I am young. I am energetic. I am vibrant. I am radiant. I am fresh. I am fearfully and wonderfully made." That's one of the best anti-aging treatments you could ever take, and it costs you nothing!

You Are an Amazing, Wonderful Masterpiece

Some people have never once said, "I am beautiful. I am attractive." They're more focused on their flaws and what they don't like about themselves and how they wish they had more here and less there. When you say, "I am beautiful," beauty comes looking for you. Youth comes looking for you. Freshness comes looking for you. Nobody else can do this for you! It has to come out of your own mouth.

Ladies, don't go around telling your husband how unattractive you are. You should never put yourself down, and especially don't put yourself down in front of your husband. You are his prize. To him you are the most beautiful woman in the world. Why would you want to tell him anything different? The last thing he needs to hear is how bad you think you look. Don't put those negative thoughts in his mind. It's not going to do him or you any good to discredit yourself. If you keep telling him how bad you look, one day he may believe you.

But when you say, "I am beautiful," not only does beauty, youth, and freshness start coming your way, but on the inside your spirit also comes alive. Your self-image begins to improve, and you'll start carrying yourself like you're someone special. You won't drag

> *Beauty is in being who God made you to be with confidence.*

through the day feeling less than or inferior. You'll have that spring in your step, that "You go, girl!" attitude. Beauty is not in how thin or tall you are, how perfect you look. Beauty is in being who God made you to be with confidence. If you're a size 4, great. If you're a size 24, great. Take what you have and make the most of it.

God made you as you are on purpose. He gave you your looks, your height, your skin color, your nose, your personality. Nothing about you is by accident. You didn't get overlooked. You didn't get left out. God calls you His masterpiece. Instead of going around feeling down on yourself, unattractive, too tall, too short, not enough of this, or too much of that, dare to get up in the morning and say, "I am a masterpiece. I am created in the image of Almighty God."

David said in Psalm 139, "God, I praise You because You have made me in an amazing way. What You have done is wonderful." Notice David's "I am"s. He was saying, not in pride but in praise to God, "I am wonderful. I am amazing. I am a masterpiece." That goes against human nature. Most of us think, *There's nothing amazing about me. Nothing wonderful. I'm just average. I'm just ordinary.* But the fact is there is nothing ordinary about you. You have a fingerprint that nobody else has. There will never be another you. Even if you have an identical twin, somebody who looks exactly like you, they don't have your same personality, your same goals, or even your same fingerprints. You are an original. When God made you, He threw away the mold. But as long as you go around thinking, *I'm just average. I'm just one of the seven billion people on the earth. There's nothing special about me,* the wrong "I am" will keep you from rising higher.

Rather than being down on ourselves and discrediting who we are and focusing on all of our flaws, I wonder what would happen if all through the day—not in front of other people but in private—we were to be as bold as David was and say, "I am amazing. I am wonderful. I am valuable." When you talk like that, amazing comes chasing you down. Awesome starts heading in your direction. You won't have that weak,

> *Be as bold as David was and say, "I am amazing. I am wonderful. I am valuable."*

defeated "I'm just average" mentality. You'll carry yourself like a king, like a queen. Not in pride. Not being better than somebody, but with a quiet confidence, with the knowledge that you've been handpicked by the Creator of the universe and you have something amazing to offer this world.

God Can Even Change Your Name

That's what happened to a lady in the Scripture named Sarai. She had to change her "I am." God promised Sarai and her husband, Abram, that they would have a baby. But Sarai was eighty years old, way past the childbearing years. Back in those days, if a wife couldn't conceive and give her husband a child for some reason, even if it was the husband's fault, the wife was considered to be a failure. She was looked down on greatly. There was a sense of shame in not being able to conceive a baby. This is how Sarai felt. She was eighty years old and never had a baby. She felt as though she had let Abram down. Her self-esteem was so low. I can imagine some of her "I am"s: "I am a failure. I am inferior. I am not good enough. I am unattractive."

Yet Sarai has this promise from God that as an older woman she was going to have a baby. God knew that it would never come to pass unless He could convince Sarai to change her "I am"s. It was so imperative that she have this new mindset that God actually changed her name from *Sarai* to *Sarah*, which means "princess."

Now every time someone said, "Good morning, Sarah," they were saying, "Good morning, Princess."

"How are you, Sarah?" "How are you, Princess?"

"Would you pass me the ketchup, Sarah?" "Would you pass me the ketchup, Princess?"

She heard this over and over. Those words got inside her and began to change her self-image. Sarah went from "I am a failure" to "I am a princess." From "I am unattractive" to "I am beautiful." From "I am ashamed" to "I am crowned by Almighty God." Instead of hanging her head in defeat, in embarrassment, she started holding her head up high. From "I'm not good enough" to "I am a child of the Most High God." From "I'm inferior" to "I am fearfully and wonderfully made." Her new attitude became: "I am amazing. I am wonderful. I am a masterpiece."

And ladies, as was true for Sarah, you may have had a lot of things in life try to push you down—bad breaks and disappointments, maybe people have even tried to make you feel as though you just don't measure up or you're not quite attractive enough. You could easily let that seed get inside, ruin your sense of value, and cause you to live inferior. But God is saying to you what He said to Sarai, "I want you to change your name to Princess"—not literally, but in your attitude. You have to shake off the negative things people have said about you. Shake off the low self-esteem and the inferiority and start carrying yourself like a princess. Start walking like a princess. Start talking like a princess. Start thinking like a princess. Start waving like a princess!

Instead of whispering, "I am inferior. I am less than," you start declaring, "I am one of a kind. I am handpicked by Almighty God. I am valuable. I am a masterpiece." When you get up in the morning, don't focus on all your flaws. Look in the mirror and dare to say, "I am beautiful. I am young. I am vibrant. I am confident. I am secure." You may have had some disappointments. People may have tried to push you down, but quit telling yourself you're all washed up. Do as Sarah and say, "I am royalty. I am crowned with favor. I am excited about my future." This princess spirit got inside Sarah. It changed her self-image. I've learned you have to change on the inside before you'll see change on the outside. At ninety-one years old, against all odds, she gave birth to that baby. The promise came to pass.

So What's Coming Out of Your Mouth?

My question today is, What kind of "I am"s are coming out of your mouth? "I am victorious. I am blessed. I am talented. I am anointed." When you have the right "I am"s, you're inviting the goodness of God. Maybe if you would just change the "I am," you would rise to a new level. Words have creative power. They can be very helpful, like electricity. Used the right way, electricity powers lights, air-conditioning, and all kinds of good things.

> *My question is, What kind of "I am"s are coming out of your mouth?*

But electricity used the wrong way can be very dangerous. It can harm you, even kill you. It's the same way with our words. Proverbs 18:21 says, "Life and death are in the power of our tongue." It's up to you to choose what follows the "I am." My encouragement is to never say negative things about yourself. Most of us would never go up to another person, at least to their face, and criticize them, yet we have no problem criticizing ourselves. "I am so slow. I am so unattractive. I am so undisciplined." That is cursing your future. Do yourself a favor and zip that up. We have enough in life against us already. Don't be against yourself.

I had a friend with whom I used to play basketball. When he would miss an important shot, he would exclaim, "I'm an idiot! I'm an idiot! I'm an idiot!" I heard that month after month. He didn't realize it, but "idiot" was coming, looking for him. I hate to say it, but I think it found him!

If you go around saying, "I am so dumb," this may be poor English, but "dumbness" is coming your way. "I am so unattractive. I am so plain." Ugliness says, "I hear somebody calling my name." Use your words to bless your future, not curse your future.

The Scripture says, "Let the weak say, 'I am strong'"—not the opposite, "I am so tired. I am so run-down." That's calling in the wrong things.

Let the poor say, "I am well off"—not, "I am broke. I am so in debt."

Let the sick say, "I am healthy. I am improving. I am getting better and better."

You Are Who God Says You Are

Romans 4 says to "call the things that are not as though they were." That simply means that you shouldn't talk about the way you are. Talk about the way you want to be. If you're struggling in your finances, don't go around saying, "Oh, man, business is so slow. The economy is so down. It's never going to work out." That's calling the things that are as if they will always be that way. That's just describing the situation. By faith you have to say, "I am blessed. I am successful. I am surrounded by God's favor."

I asked a young man recently how he was doing in high school. He said, "I'm doing okay. I'm just a C student." Come to find out, when he was back in elementary school, one of his teachers told him he was a C student, and he let that seed take root and bloom. I told him what I'm telling you. As long as you're saying, "I am a C student," you're not going to become an A student. You're calling in the C's, and those C's will come find you wherever you go. If you're not careful, you'll make a C in homeroom, a C in lunch, and a C in PE. Change the "I am." "I am an A student. I am smart. I am full of wisdom. I am a good learner. I am excellent."

Have you allowed what somebody—a coach, a teacher, a parent, an ex-spouse—said about you to hold you back? They've planted negative seeds of what you cannot do. "You're not smart enough. You're not talented enough. You're not disciplined enough. You're not attractive enough. You'll always make C's. You'll always be mediocre. You'll always struggle with your weight." Get rid of those lies! That is not who you are. You are who God says you are.

People may have tried to push you down and tell you who or what you can't become. Let that go in one ear and out the other ear. What somebody said about you doesn't determine your destiny: *God does.* You need to know not only who you are but also who you are not. In other words, "I am not who people say I am. I am who God says I am. I am not the tail; I am the head. I am not a borrower; I am a lender. I am not cursed; I am blessed."

> *What somebody said about you doesn't determine your destiny:* God does.

As was true in this young man's life, somebody may have spoken negative words to you when you were young. But know this: Before anyone could put a curse on you, God put a blessing on you. Before you were formed in your mother's womb, God knew you, and He approved you. When God made you, He stepped back and said, "I like that. That was good. Another masterpiece!" He stamped His approval on you. Other people may try to disapprove of you. Don't go around feeling less than, feeling inferior. Our attitude should be: *I am approved by Almighty God. I am accepted. I am a master-piece.* When you talk like that, the seeds of greatness God has placed inside will begin to spring forth.

Change Your "I Am"s

You have gifts and talents that you've not tapped into yet. There is a treasure inside you. Throughout life, negative thoughts will try to keep it pushed down. The enemy doesn't want you to reach your full potential. There are forces constantly trying to make you feel intimidated, inferior, unqualified. If you're going to fulfill your destiny, you have to shake off the negative voices. Shake off the thoughts that are telling you, *I am unable. I am unqualified.* Don't invite weakness. Don't give intimidation an invitation. You may feel unqualified, but before you were born, God equipped you. He empowered you. You are not lacking anything. God has already stamped His approval on you. People may try to push you down, but when you know God has approved you, you realize, *I don't need other people's*

> *When you know God has approved you, you realize,* I don't need other people's approval. I've been equipped, empowered, and anointed by the Creator of the universe!

approval. I've been equipped, empowered, and anointed by the Creator of the universe!

I know a man who was told by his high school counselor that he wasn't very smart and should focus on the lowest skilled job that he could find. I'm sure the counselor meant well, but he didn't know who this young man was on the inside. He didn't see the seeds of greatness God had planted in this young man. As a high school student, this young man's "I am" was distorted. "I am not up to par. I am not smart. I am very average." He didn't realize he was inviting that into his life, but over time it showed up.

After high school, this man got a job at the local factory and stayed at the lowest level year after year after year. One day the factory closed down, so he went across town and applied at another factory. This company had a policy that job applicants had to first take an IQ test. He took the test and scored the highest in the company's sixty-three-year history. His IQ score was assessed at genius level. He went on to start his own business, and he invented and patented two very successful products. Today, he is extremely blessed.

What happened? He changed his "I am."

Could it be what someone has told you is keeping you from God's best? Could it be that the wrong "I am" is keeping you from rising higher and reaching your full potential? Do what this man did. Change your "I am." Don't let what somebody told you determine your destiny. Get in agreement with God. Know who you are and know who you are not. "I am not lacking. I am not average. I am not inferior. I am equipped. I am empowered. I am anointed. I am wise. I am a masterpiece."

Be a Joshua, Be a Caleb

In Numbers 13, Moses sent twelve men in to spy out the Promised
Land. After forty days, ten of them came back and said, "Moses,
we don't have a chance. The cities are fortified and very large and
the people are huge. Compared to them we felt like we were grasshoppers." Notice their "I am"s. "I am weak. I am inferior. I am
intimidated. I am afraid." What happened? Fear, intimidation, and
inferiority came knocking at their door.

The other two spies, Joshua and Caleb, came back with a different report. They said, "Moses, yes, the people are big, but we know
our God is much bigger. We are well able. Let us go in and take the
land at once." Their "I am"s were just the opposite. "I am strong. I
am equipped. I am confident. I am more than a conqueror."

What is interesting is that the negative report from the ten spies
spread like wildfire throughout the rest of the camp. Before long
some two million people were intimidated and afraid. Nobody even
paid attention to Joshua and Caleb's report of faith. Here's what
I've learned: A negative report always spreads faster than a positive
report. When people are murmuring, complaining, and talking
defeat, be on guard. Make sure you don't let the wrong "I am" take
root.

The people of Israel were so distressed by the negative report that
they complained against Moses and Aaron, "Why did you even
bring us out here? We're going to die in the wilderness. Our children, our wives, they're going to be taken as plunder."

God answered back something very powerful and very sobering.
He said in Numbers 14, "I will do for you exactly what you have
said. You said you're going to die in the wilderness, so you will die in
the wilderness." God is saying the same thing to us. "I am going to

do exactly what you've been saying." Don't ever say, "I am weak. I'm intimidated. I'm inferior." Friend, the wrong "I am" can keep you from your destiny.

Do you remember reading in the Scripture about a man named Sethur, a man named Gaddi, or a man named Shaphat? I'm fairly certain that you've never heard of them. You know why? They were listed among the ten spies who brought the negative report. They also never made it into the Promised Land. The fact is they were called to be history makers, just as Joshua and Caleb were. They had seeds of greatness inside them, but the wrong "I am" kept them from making their mark.

Don't let that be your destiny. You may be facing some major obstacles. My challenge is for you to be a Joshua. Be a Caleb. "I am strong. I am confident. I am equipped. I am more than a conqueror. I am well able." Make sure you have the right "I am"s coming out of your mouth.

Joshua and Caleb were the only two from that whole wilderness company to ever make it into the Promised Land.

Speak These "I Am"s over Your Life

Let me give you some "I am"s to speak over your life. Read over these declarations every day. Get them down in your spirit. Meditate on them. They may not all be true right now, but as you continue to speak them, they will become a reality.

"I am blessed. I am prosperous. I am successful."

"I am victorious. I am talented. I am creative."

"I am wise. I am healthy. I am in shape."

"I am energetic. I am happy. I am positive."

"I am passionate. I am strong. I am confident."

"I am secure. I am beautiful. I am attractive."

"I am valuable. I am free. I am redeemed."

"I am forgiven. I am anointed. I am accepted."

"I am approved. I am prepared. I am qualified."

"I am motivated. I am focused. I am disciplined."

"I am determined. I am patient. I am kind."

"I am generous. I am excellent. I am equipped."

"I am empowered. I am well able."

"I am a child of the Most High God."

CHAPTER TWO

Be Positive or Be Quiet

You are where you are today in part because of what you've been saying about yourself. Words are like seeds. When you speak something out, you give life to what you're saying. If you continue to say it, eventually that can become a reality. Whether you realize it or not, you are prophesying your future. This is great when we're saying things such as, "I am

> *Words are like seeds. When you speak something out, you give life to what you're saying.*

blessed. I am strong. I will accomplish my dreams. I'm coming out of debt." That's not just being positive; you are actually prophesying victory, prophesying success, prophesying new levels. Your life will move in the direction of your words.

But too many people go around prophesying just the opposite. "I never get any good breaks." "I'll never get back in shape." "Business is slow. I'll probably get laid off." "Flu season is here. I always get it." They don't realize they are prophesying defeat. It's just like they're calling in bad breaks, mediocrity, and lack.

The Scripture says, "We will eat the fruit of our words." When you talk, you are planting seeds. At some point, you're going to eat that fruit. My challenge is: Make sure you're planting the right kind of seeds. If you want apples, you have to sow apple seeds. If you want oranges, you can't plant cactus seeds, poison ivy seeds, or mushroom seeds. You're going to reap fruit from the exact seeds that you've been sowing. In other words, you can't talk negative and expect to live a positive life. You can't talk defeat and expect to have victory. You can't talk lack, not enough, can't afford it, never get ahead and expect to have abundance. If you have a poor mouth, you're going to have a poor life.

If you don't like what you're seeing, start sowing some different seeds. Instead of saying, "I'll never get well, Joel. This sickness has been in my family for three generations," plant the right seeds by stating, "God is restoring health back unto me. This sickness didn't come to stay; it came to pass. I'm getting better and better every day." You keep sowing those positive seeds and eventually you'll eat that abundant fruit—health, wholeness, victory.

Instead of saying, "I'll never get out of debt. I'll never rise any higher," you start speaking the promises of God: "I will lend and not borrow. Whatever I touch prospers and succeeds. I'm coming into overflow, into more than enough." Start sowing seeds of increase, seeds of abundance. No more "I'll never accomplish my dreams." Instead, "I have the favor of God. Blessings are chasing me down. The right people are searching me out. New opportunities, new levels are in my future." If you'll keep talking like that, you'll reap a harvest of good things.

Start Blessing Your Life

The Scripture talks about how with our tongue we can bless our life or we can curse our life. Many people don't realize they're cursing their future with their words. Every time you say, "I never get any good breaks," you just cursed your life. "I'll never be able to afford that nice house." "I'll never be able to break this addiction." "I'll never meet the right person." No; stop cursing your future. Sometimes the enemy doesn't have to defeat us; we defeat ourselves. Pay attention to what you're saying. Are you blessing your life? Or are you cursing it?

> *Pay attention to what you're saying. Are you blessing your life? Or are you cursing it?*

I had a classmate in high school who was always very negative even though he was one of the stars on our football team, was always in great shape, and had thick, curly hair. Every time I asked him what was going on, he gave this standard reply: "Not much. I'm just getting old, fat, and bald." I must have heard him say that five hundred times. I know he was just kind of kidding, but I wouldn't kid about that. About fifteen years later, when I ran into him at the mall, I nearly passed out. He had prophesied his future. He looked old, fat, and bald. Don't speak that defeat over your life. Our attitude should be, *I'm getting younger. God is renewing my youth like the eagles. I'm getting stronger, healthier, better looking. I'm going to keep my hair. I'm going to stay in my right mind. I'm going to live a long, productive, faith-filled life.* Don't go around cursing your future. Start blessing your life. Prophesy good things.

I know this man who was concerned that he was going to get Alzheimer's disease because several people in his family had it—a grandfather, a great-uncle. This man was only in his early fifties, but he constantly kept bringing up what might happen. He told me that he was actually making plans for someone to take care of him, getting everything lined up. Of course, it's good to use common sense, to be wise, and to plan ahead in your life where you can. But if you go around talking about when you're going to get a disease and making plans for it, you probably won't be disappointed. You're calling it in. Just like you're sending it an invitation.

I told this man what I'm telling you: "Don't say another time that you're going to have Alzheimer's or any other disease. Start declaring, 'No weapon formed against me will ever prosper. I will live out my days in good health, with a clear mind, with good memory, with clarity of thought. My mind is alert. My senses are sharp. My youth is being renewed.'" You must prophesy health. Prophesy a long, productive life. Your words will become your reality.

Don't Get Trapped by Your Own Words

Proverbs 6:2 states, "We are snared by the words of our mouth." *Snared* means "to be trapped." Your words can trap you. What you say can cause you to stumble and keep you from your potential. You're not snared by what you think. Negative thoughts come to us all. But when you speak them out loud, you give them life. That's when they become a reality. If you say, "I'll never get back in shape," it becomes more difficult to get back in shape. You just made it harder. When you say, "I never get any good breaks," you stop the favor that was ordained to you. If you say, "I'm not that talented. I don't have a good personality," you're calling in mediocrity. It's setting the limits for your life. When negative thoughts come, the key is to never verbalize them. That thought will die stillborn if you don't speak it.

> *When negative thoughts come, the key is to never verbalize them.*

When we acquired the former Compaq Center, it was a dream

come true. We were so excited. Our architects drew up plans to change it from a basketball arena to a church. They called us together and said it was going to cost a hundred million dollars to renovate! After they picked me up off the floor, my first thoughts were, *That's impossible! There's no way! I've only been the pastor four years. They cannot expect me to raise those kinds of funds.* Even though those thoughts were racing through my mind again and again, I knew enough to keep my mouth closed. I kept a big smile on my face and acted as though it was no big deal. I knew if I didn't verbalize those negative thoughts, eventually they would die stillborn. It's one thing to think that something's impossible, but when you start telling people something's impossible, it takes on a whole new meaning.

You may think, *I'll never get that job. I'll never get well. I'll never meet the right person.* Those thoughts come to all of us. You can't stop that. My challenge is: Don't give them life by speaking them out loud. Don't go call your friends and tell them how it's not going to happen. I told our team, "I don't see a way, but I know God has a way. He didn't bring us this far to leave us." My report was: "God is supplying all of our needs. The funds are coming in. It may look impossible on paper, but with God all things are possible." I knew better than to curse my future. I didn't want to get trapped by my words. I knew if I kept prophesying the right things—increase, favor, more than enough—we would start moving toward it, and we did!

In the tough times, you have to especially be on guard. It's very tempting to vent your frustration and tell people how the loan didn't go through, how bad the medical report was, or how certain people just didn't treat you right. When you continually talk about the problem, that's going to only make you more discouraged, and it gives that problem more life. You're making it bigger. Turn it around. Don't talk about the problem; talk about the promise.

> *Don't talk about the problem; talk about the promise.*

Instead of complaining, "Oh, man, I've got this big challenge," state, "I serve a big God. He spoke worlds into existence. Nothing's too difficult for Him."

Instead of surmising, "I didn't get the promotion they promised. They passed over me again. Another disappointment," declare, "I know when one door closes that means God has something better. He's directing my steps. I'm excited about my future."

Instead of concluding, "I'll never meet the right person. I'm too old. It's been too long," state, "Something good is going to happen to me. Divine connections are coming my way."

When someone says, "I'm sorry to hear that you got a bad medical report. Is it true?" you should respond, "Yes, that's true. But I have another report that tells me God is restoring health back unto me."

If your friend remarks, "Well, I heard those people did you wrong," feel free to smile, nod your head, and explain, "Yes, but I'm not worried. God is my vindicator. He's fighting my battles. He's promised to give me beauty for ashes."

Two Voices—Which One Are You Choosing?

In life, there are always two voices competing for your attention—the voice of faith and the voice of defeat. Just as I did, you'll hear a voice piping in, "You can't possibly raise that amount of money. It's insurmountable. It's not going to work out. Just accept it." You'll be tempted to worry, to be negative, to complain. But if you listen carefully, you'll hear another voice. The voice of faith is saying, "God has a way. Favor is coming. Healing is coming. Breakthroughs are coming."

> *If you listen carefully, you'll hear another voice—the voice of faith.*

One voice will point out that you've reached your limits. You've gone as far as you can. You don't have what it takes. The other voice is clear and matter-of-fact: "You are well able. You can do all things through Christ. Your best days are still out in front of you." Now, here's the beauty. You get to choose which voice comes to life. The way you do it is by what you speak. When you verbalize that thought, you're giving it the right to come to pass. If you mope around saying, "The problem's too big. I'll never get well," you are choosing the wrong voice. You have to get in agreement with God. The other voice may seem louder, but you can override it. You can take away all of its power by choosing the voice of faith.

Maybe you're going to a job interview. One voice will warn you, "You're not going to get it. You're wasting your time. These people are not going to like you." Another voice will counter, "You have the favor of God. You're blessed. You're confident. You have what it takes." If you get up that morning and tell your spouse, "I don't think I'm going to get this job. They're not going to like me. I'm not qualified," there's no use in your going. You're being trapped by your words. You have to dig your heels in and say, "I am not giving life to any more defeat. I am not speaking lack. I'm not speaking sickness. I'm not speaking mediocrity, fear, doubt. I can't do it. I'm choosing the voice of faith. It says I am strong, I am healthy, I am blessed. I am favored. I am a victor and not a victim."

God gave Jeremiah a promise that he would become a great prophet to the nations (Jeremiah 1). But when he heard God's voice, he was very young and unsure of himself. He instead listened to the other voice and said, "God, I can't do that. I can't speak to the nations. I'm too young. I wouldn't know what to say."

God said, "Jeremiah, say not that you are too young."

The first thing God did was to stop his negative words. Why did God do that? Because He knew that if Jeremiah went around saying, "I'm not qualified. I can't do this. I don't have what it takes," he would become exactly what he was saying. So God said in effect, "Jeremiah, zip it up. You may think it, but don't speak it out loud." It goes on to tell how Jeremiah changed what he was saying, and he became a prophet to the nations. The promise came to pass.

In the same way, God has called every one of us to do something great. He's put dreams and desires inside, but it's easy to acquiesce as Jeremiah did and say, "I can't do that. I'm too young. I'm too old. I've made too many mistakes. I don't have the education. I don't have the experience." We can all make excuses, but God is saying to us what He said to Jeremiah: "Stop saying that." Don't curse your future. Those negative words can keep you from God's best.

Negative Words Stop God's Promises

Sometimes the reason a promise is being delayed is because of what we're saying. Imagine that your answer is on the way. God has already dispatched the angel with your healing, your promotion, your vindication. But right before it arrives, God says to the angel, "Hold on. Don't go any further. Stay right where you are."

The angel replies, "Why, God? This is what You promised. It's in Your Word."

God answers, "No, listen to what he's saying. He's talking about how it's not going to happen, how the problem is too big, how it's been too long, how he'll never meet the right person."

Negative words stop God's promises. I wonder how many times we're just a couple of months away from seeing the answer, a couple of months from meeting the right person. You've been praying for years that God would bring somebody great into your life. But right before that somebody shows up, you let your guard down and start saying, "Oh, it's not going to happen. I'm too old. Nobody's interested in me." God has to say to the angel, "Don't go any further."

The good news is that promise is still in your future. God didn't cancel it because you got negative. He still has the right person for you, and if you'll zip up the doubt and switch over into faith, at the right time, that person will show up. God will release what negative words have delayed. God still has your healing, your promotion, your restoration. Now do your part. Quit talking about how it's not going to happen. You may not see a way, but God still has a way. It may look impossible, but God can do the impossible. Just because you don't see anything happening doesn't mean God is not working. Right now, behind the scenes, God is arranging things in your favor. He is lining up the right people. He is moving the wrong people out of the way. He is positioning you exactly where He wants you to be. Now don't delay the promise by speaking negative words.

When our son, Jonathan, was seventeen years old, we were in the process of applying to different colleges. Some schools accept only 5 percent of the students who apply. That means, of course, that 95 percent of the applicants get turned down. It's easy to think, *Why do we even want to apply to those schools? It's practically impossible to get in. More than nine out of ten students get denied. Jonathan, don't get your hopes up. I don't see how you could get in there.*

If we're not careful, we'll talk ourselves out of it. You may think those thoughts, but don't make the mistake of verbalizing them. Learn to turn it around. "God, I know You have my son in the palm of Your hand. You've already picked out the right college for him to attend. There may be only a 5 percent chance for some schools, but God, I know that with You there's a 100 percent chance he will get in exactly where You want him to go. God, You control the whole universe."

That's much better than going around saying, "All the odds are against me. It doesn't look good. I don't see how it's going to happen." No, zip that up. If you can't be positive, at least be quiet. Your words prophesy your future. If you say, "I'll never get in," you're right; you'll never get in. If you say, "This problem is going to sink me," it will take you under. If you say, "I'll never be able to afford a nice house," you'll never be able to afford a nice house. You're being snared by the words of your mouth.

Put a Watch over Your Mouth

In the first chapter of Luke, an angel appeared to a priest named Zachariah while he was serving in the temple. The angel told him that his wife, Elizabeth, was going to have a baby and they were to name him John. Zachariah was very surprised, because he and his wife were way up there in years. He said to the angel, "Are you sure this is going to happen? It sounds great, but do you see how old we are? To me, it just doesn't seem possible."

The angel said, "Zachariah, I am Gabriel. I stand in the presence of Almighty God, and what God says will come to pass."

God knows the power of our words. He knew that if Zachariah went around speaking defeat, it would stop His plan. So God did something unusual. The angel said, "Zachariah, because you doubted, you will remain silent and not be able to speak until the baby is born." Zachariah left the temple unable to talk; he couldn't speak one word for nine months, until that baby was born.

Why did God take away Zachariah's speech? God knew he would go out and start telling his friends how it wasn't going to happen. "Hey, man. This angel appeared and said we're going to have a baby. He must have the wrong person. We're too old." Those negative words would have stopped his destiny. That's why the Scripture says, "Put a watch over your mouth." In other words, "Be careful what you allow to come out of your mouth."

"I don't think I'm ever going to get well. I've had this sickness for three years." No; put a watch over your mouth. Don't prophesy defeat. If you're going to say anything, declare what God says: "I will live and not die. God is restoring health back unto me. The number of my days He will fulfill." All through the day you need to ask yourself, "Is what I'm about to say what I want to come into my life?" Because what you're saying, you're inviting in.

When you say, "I'll never pay off my house and get out of debt. The economy is too slow," you're inviting struggle and lack. When you say, "My career has dead-ended. This is as good as it gets," you're inviting defeat and mediocrity. You need to send out some new invitations. When you say, "I will lend and not borrow. God's favor surrounds me like a shield. Whatever I touch prospers and succeeds," you are inviting increase, good breaks, and success. When you say, "I will overcome this problem. I am more than a conqueror. If God be for me, who dare be against me?" you're inviting strength, healing, restoration, vindication, and breakthroughs.

Pay attention to what you're inviting. "I'll never pass this algebra course. I've never been good in math. I just don't understand it." Change the invitation. "I can do all things through Christ. I have good understanding. I am full of wisdom. I am an A student." When you do that, you're inviting wisdom

> *Pay attention to what you're inviting into your life.*

and an acceleration of knowledge. You're inviting God's blessings. Make sure you're sending out the right invitations.

When I first started ministering back in 1999, I had never done this before, and I was very nervous and unsure of myself. Negative thoughts bombarded my mind: *Joel, you're going to get up there and make a fool of yourself. You're not going to know what to say. Nobody is going to listen to you. Why should they? You don't have the experience.* All through the day I had to ignore those thoughts. I would go around saying under my breath, "I am anointed. I am equipped. I am strong in the Lord." Before I would come to church and minister, I would look at myself in the mirror and say, "Joel, you are well able. You've been raised up for such a time as this."

I didn't feel confident, but I called myself confident. I didn't feel anointed, but I called myself anointed. You may not feel blessed, but you need to call yourself blessed. The circumstances may not say you're prosperous, but by faith you need to call yourself prosperous. You may not feel healthy today, but don't go around telling everyone how you're not going to make it. Start calling yourself healthy, whole, strong, full of energy and full of life.

When Marching Around Walls, Zip It Up

When Joshua was leading the people of Israel toward the Promised Land, they came to the city of Jericho. It towered between them and their destiny. They couldn't go around it. They had to go through it. The problem was: Jericho was surrounded by huge, thick, tall walls made of stone and mortar. It didn't look as though there was any way the Israelites could get in. But God told them to do something that sounded strange—for six days they were to march around those walls once a day, and on the seventh day they were to march around them seven times. As if that wasn't odd enough, God gave them one final instruction, which was the key to the whole plan working. He said, "While you're marching around the walls, I don't want you to say one word, not a whisper, not a short conversation, not an update on how it's going. Keep totally silent."

Why did God not allow them to speak? God knew that after a couple of times around the perimeter of the walls, if not before they even started marching, they would be saying, "What in the world are we doing out here? These walls are never going to fall. Look how thick they are. They've been here forever. Joshua must have heard God wrong." Somebody else speaks up, "Yeah, and I'm tired. I'm hot. I'm hungry. This dust is getting in my face." God knew they would talk themselves out of it. There are times in all of our lives when it's difficult to be positive. And that's okay. Just stay silent. Don't tell everyone what you're thinking. The people of Israel marched in silence, and you know how the story ends. On the seventh time around on the seventh day the walls came tumbling down.

Here's the question today: Could it be that negative words are keeping you out of your Promised Land? Could it be that if you would remain silent, that if you would zip it up and not talk about how big the problem is, not complain about what didn't work out, not tell a friend how you're never going to be successful, maybe the walls that are holding you back would come down? Imagine behind those walls are your healing, your promotion, your dream coming to pass. Every day, so to speak, you're walking around the walls. What are you saying? "This wall is never going to fall, Joel. I've had this addiction since high school." "I'll never be able to start my own business. I don't know the right people."

God is saying to us what He said to the Israelites: "If you can't say anything positive and full of faith, don't say anything at all." Don't let your negative words keep you from God's best. If you'll stop talking defeat, lack, how it's not going to happen, and simply remain silent, God can do for you what He did for them. He knows how to bring those walls down.

When we're marching around the walls, sometimes we go day after day and don't see anything happening. Just like the Israelites, the thoughts come swirling around our heads: *You didn't hear God right. Nothing is changing. You go to work every week and do your best, but you're not being promoted, and it's never going to happen.* No, that is a time of testing. Like the Israelites, you're marching around the walls. You may be on day five, day six. That simply means you've been doing it a year, two years, or five years. You've thought surely it would have happened by now.

Pass that test. Don't start complaining. Don't do like the first group that stopped at the door of the Promised Land and said, "Oh, what's the use? Let's just settle here." When the negative thoughts come, let them die stillborn. Refuse to prophesy defeat over your life. If you do this,

> *Pass that test. Don't start complaining.*

you will come into your seventh day. Like what happened with the Israelites, those walls will come tumbling down. God is a faithful God. He will do what He has promised you.

"It Is Well"

In II Kings 4, there is a story of a woman who was a good friend of the prophet Elisha. In fact, she had built an extra room on her house, so when Elisha was in town he could come and stay there. One day Elisha asked her what he could do for her to return the favor. She said, "Nothing, Elisha. My husband and I are doing just fine."

Elisha's assistant brought it to his attention that the couple didn't have any children. Her husband was an older man. Before Elisha left the woman, he prophesied, "By this time next year you're going to have a baby." She was so excited. It seemed too good to be true. But the next year, just like he told her, she had a son. When the boy was around ten years old, he was out in the field playing and his head began to hurt very badly. They carried him home and placed him in his mother's arms where he later died. You can imagine how this mother felt. She was heartbroken, devastated beyond measure. She carried her son to Elisha's room and placed him on Elisha's bed.

For most people this would be the end of the story, but not for this lady. She asked for a donkey and said, "I'm going to see the prophet Elisha." She told her assistant to ride fast and not slow down unless he was told. When Elisha saw the dust billowing up in the sky a couple of miles away, he noticed it was his friend, the woman who had built the extra room on her house for him. Elisha told his assistant Gehazi, "Go find out what's wrong."

Gehazi ran to meet the woman way down the road, stopped her, and said, "Elisha is concerned. Why are you coming unexpectedly in such a hurry? Is it well with you? Is it well with your husband? Is it well with the child?"

Speaking words of faith, she simply replied, "It is well," and kept heading full steam ahead.

Think of all the negative thoughts that this woman was fighting, and then consider her actual words. A lot of times when we face difficulties and somebody asks us how everything is going, we do just the opposite and tell them everything that's wrong. It's easy to talk about the problem, how bad it is, how it's never going to work out. But in those tough times—when you feel like complaining, when you've got a good reason to be sour, because you lost a job, or a friend did you wrong, or you're not feeling well—you have to dig your heels in and say it by faith: "Business is slow, but all is well. God is still on the throne. He's the Lord my Provider." Or, "The medical report wasn't good, but all is well. God is my healer. Nothing will snatch me out of His hands."

She finally made it to Elisha's house and told him the son he promised her had died. Elisha went and prayed for the boy, and he came back to life. What I want you to see is that in her darkest hour, even when it looked impossible, this lady refused to get negative and speak defeat. When Gehazi asked, "Is everything okay?" she could have spoken out loud what I'm sure she was thinking, "No! I'm in the midst of a great tragedy. I'm facing the biggest challenge of my life." Nobody would have faulted her for that. But she chose to speak faith even though her mind was being bombarded with doubt. She had a watch over her mouth. She wasn't going to be snared by her words.

When you're hurting, you've been through a disappointment, and you've suffered a loss, you have to do what she did. Say it by faith:

> Say it by faith: "All is well."

"All is well." It may not look well. It may not feel well. In the natural you should be complaining, talking about how bad it is, but instead you're making a declaration of faith: "All is well." That's when the most powerful force in the universe goes to work.

Every Wall Will Come Tumbling Down

God can resurrect dead dreams. He can resurrect a dead marriage. He can resurrect health that's going down or a business that's failing. When you get in agreement with God, all things are possible. You may be facing a big obstacle. It doesn't look good. But here's a key: Don't talk about the size of your problem. Talk about the size of your God. God stopped the sun for Joshua. He parted the Red Sea for the Israelites. He breathed new life into this mother's little boy. He can turn your situation around as well. He can make a way even though you don't see a way.

My challenge to you today is: Don't let your negative words stop what God wants to do. If you can't say anything positive, zip it up. You may think it, but don't give it life by speaking it out. Your healing, your vindication, and your promotion are right up in front of you. As was true

> *If you can't say anything positive, zip it up.*

of Jeremiah, God has already ordained you to do something great. Now, put a watch over your mouth. Pay attention to what you're saying.

When you make this adjustment, God is going to release promises that have been delayed. Suddenly the things you've been praying about—breaking that addiction, meeting the right person, getting healthy again, starting that business—are going to fall into place. You're going to see God's favor in a new way. He's going to open up new doors of opportunity just as He did for Joshua and the Israelites. I believe and declare that every wall that's holding you back is about to come tumbling down. You and your family will make it into your Promised Land!

CHAPTER THREE

Say So

Words have creative power. When you speak something out, you give life to what you're saying. It's one thing to believe that you're blessed. That's important. But when you say, "I am blessed," it takes on a whole new meaning. That's when blessings come looking for you. The Scripture says, "Let the redeemed of the Lord *say so*."

> *If you're going to go to the next level, you have to say so.*

It doesn't say, "Let the redeemed think so, or believe so, or hope so." That's all good, but you have to take it one step further and *say so*. If you're going to go to the next level, you have to *say so*. If you're going to accomplish a dream, overcome an obstacle, or break an addiction, you have to start declaring it. It has to come out of your mouth. That's how you give life to your faith.

When God created the worlds, He didn't just think them into being. He didn't just believe there would be light and land and oceans and animals. He had it in His heart, but nothing happened until He spoke. He said, "Let there be light," and light came. His thoughts didn't set it into motion; His words set it into motion. It's the same principle today. You can believe all day long and not see anything happen. You can have faith in your heart, big dreams, be standing on God's promises, and never see anything change. What's the problem? Nothing happens until you speak. Instead of just believing you're going to get out of debt, you have to say so. Declare every day, "I am coming out of debt. I am the head and not the tail. God's favor

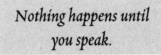

Nothing happens until you speak.

surrounds me like a shield." When you speak, just like when God spoke, things begin to happen. Opportunities will find you. Good breaks, promotion, and ideas will track you down.

Instead of just thinking, *I hope I get over this illness. I'm praying I'll get better*, which is good, you have to take it one more step and start declaring it. "I am strong. I am healthy. I will live and not die. With long life God is going to satisfy me." That's what activates your faith. It's not just hoping you have a good year or just hoping that you accomplish your dreams. Hope is good, but nothing happens until you speak. Before you leave the house every day, declare it: "This is going to be my best year. Things have shifted in my favor. I'm going to a new level." When you talk like that, the angels go to work, opening up new doors, lining up the right people, and arranging things in your favor.

"I Will Say"

Psalm 91 says, "I will say of the Lord, 'He is my refuge, my fortress, and my shield.'" The next verse says, "He will deliver me, protect me, and cover me." Notice the connection. *I will say* and *He will do*. It doesn't say, "I believe He is my refuge. I believe He will be my strength." The psalmist went around declaring it, speaking it out: "The Lord is my refuge. The Lord is my strength." Notice what happened. God became his refuge and strength. God was saying in effect, "If you're bold enough to speak it, I'm bold enough to do it."

Have you ever declared that your dreams are coming to pass? Have you ever said, "I will pay off my house." "I will start my own business." "I will get my degree." "I will lose this weight." "I will see my family restored"? Whatever God has put in your heart, it needs to get in your conversation. Talk like it's going to happen. Talk like it's already on the way: "When I get married... When I graduate from college... When I see my family restored..." Not *if* it's going to happen, but *when* it's going to happen. That's your faith being released.

One of our staff members had been trying for more than ten years to have a baby, with no success. One day we were in a staff meeting, planning out the next year. She made the statement, "When I have my baby, I'm going to be out for a couple of months. We'll have to find somebody to fill in." I thought she was pregnant and that nobody had told me, so I didn't act surprised or say anything. My sister Lisa was in the meeting as well. I asked her afterward, "Why didn't you tell me she was pregnant?"

She said, "Joel, she's not pregnant. She just talks like it's going to happen."

This went on for years. "When I have my baby... When I get pregnant... When my child shows up..." What was she doing? Saying so. She didn't just believe it. She was declaring it. In the natural, she was getting too old to have a baby. Her doctors told her it wasn't going to happen. It looked impossible. Most people would have given up and accepted it. But not this lady. She kept saying so, kept declaring it: "When my baby shows up..." Twenty years later, she gave birth not to one baby but to two. She had twins. She declared of the Lord, and God did what He promised.

But think about the opposite of Psalm 91: "I will not say of the Lord, and He will not do." That's the principle. Nothing happens until you speak.

What Are You Saying?

When we were trying to acquire the Compaq Center to become our church building, Victoria and I would drive around it night after night and say, "That's our building. Father, thank You for fighting our battles. Lord, thank You that You are making a way where we don't see a way." We didn't just think about it, pray about it, or believe that it would happen. That's all important, but we took one more step and declared that it was ours. It became a part of our everyday conversation. At the dinner table: "When we get the Compaq Center, we could do this. When we renovate it...When we move in... When we have the grand opening..." Not "I don't know, Victoria. It's going to be very expensive. Where are we going to get the funds? The opponents, they're really strong." No, we said of the Lord, as the psalmist did, "God, we know You are bigger than any obstacle. We know You are

> *We declared it, and God did it.*

supplying all of our needs. Lord, we know if You be for us, who dare be against us?" We declared it, and God did it.

What are you saying of the Lord? "Well, Joel. My problems are really big today. My dreams look impossible. My marriage is so messed up. We'll never be restored." Don't talk about how big your problem is. Talk about how big your God is. When you say of the Lord, "You're my healer, my way maker, my dream giver, my restorer, my vindicator, my health, my peace, my victory," that's when God will show up and do more than you can ask or think.

I have some friends who were believing to have another child. They have a daughter, but they really wanted to have a son. Every time the wife got pregnant, she had a miscarriage. This happened five times in nine years. They were very discouraged and tempted to give up. The husband's name is Joe and had gone by Joe his whole life. But one day he read that his full name—Joseph—means "God will add." When he understood that, something came alive inside. He knew God was saying, "I'm going to add to you a son." He remembered the story in the Scripture where God changed Abram's name to Abraham, which means "father of many nations." God gave Abraham a child, a son, at a very old age when it looked impossible. Joe decided to go back to using his original name. He told his family, his friends, and coworkers, "Don't call me Joe anymore. Call me Joseph."

They thought he was having a midlife crisis. But every time someone said, "Hello, Joseph," they were saying, "God will add." They were speaking victory over his life. He kept saying so, declaring it. About six months later, his wife became pregnant with a baby boy. For the first time in ten years, she carried the baby to full term. Their son was born healthy and whole. As a testimony to God's goodness, they named that little boy Joseph: "God will add."

Whatever God Has Put in Your Heart

Are you declaring victory over your life, over your family, over your career? Nothing happens until you speak. When you get up in the morning, you need to make some declarations of faith. Whatever God has put in your heart, declare that it will come to pass. I say every day, "I am increasing in the anointing, in wisdom, in favor, and in influence. Every message is getting better. God is taking our ministry where no ministry has ever gone." You have to speak favor into your future. I declare every day, "My children will fulfill their destinies. Their gifts and talents will come out to the full. They will supersede anything that we've done."

Ever since I took over for my father in the church, I have said, "When people turn me on, on television, they cannot turn me off." Do you know how many letters I get from people who say, "Joel, I was flipping through the channels. I don't like TV preachers. I never watch TV preachers, but when I turned you on, I couldn't turn you off"?

I think to myself, *I called you in! I said so.*

One man wrote and told how his wife tried to get him to watch the program for many years, but he wouldn't do it. One day he was flipping through the channels and came across our program. Normally he would flip by it very quickly. But for some reason this day his remote control stopped working, and he got stuck on our program. He was so frustrated. He finagled with the remote and ended up changing the batteries. It still wouldn't work. He said, "Joel, even though I tried to act like I wasn't listening, you were speaking directly to me." The funny thing is, when our program was over, the remote control went back to working just fine. He said, "Now I never miss one of your programs."

When you declare favor over your life and over your future, God will make things happen that should have never happened. Our attitude should be, *I'm coming out of debt, and I'm saying so. This will be my best year, and I'm saying so. I will overcome every obstacle, and I'm saying so. I will accomplish my dreams, and I'm saying so.*

Use Your Words to Change
the Situation

In the Scripture there was a lady who had been sick for many years. She had gone to the best doctors, spent all of her money trying to get well, but nothing worked. One day she heard Jesus was coming through town. The Scripture says, *"She kept saying to herself."* She wasn't saying, "I'm never going to get well. I can't believe this has happened to me. I always get bad breaks." No, she kept saying to herself, "When I get to Jesus, I know I will be made whole." In the midst of the difficulty, she was prophesying victory. All through the day, over and over, she kept saying, "Healing is on its way. Brighter days are up ahead." When she started making her way to Jesus, it was extremely crowded, but she didn't complain, she didn't get discouraged, and she kept saying, "This is my time. Things are changing in my favor." The more she said it, the closer she got. Finally she reached out and touched the edge of His robe, and she was instantly healed.

Notice the principle: Whatever you're constantly saying, you're moving toward. You may be struggling in your finances, but when

> *Whatever you're constantly saying, you're moving toward.*

you keep declaring, "I am blessed. I am prosperous. I have the favor of God," every time you say it, you're moving toward increase. You're getting closer to seeing that come to pass. You may be facing a sickness. It doesn't look good. But every time you declare, "I am healthy. I am strong. I am getting better," you're moving toward health, wholeness, victory. Perhaps you're struggling with an addiction. Every time you declare, "I am free. This addiction does not control me," you're moving toward freedom. You're moving toward breakthroughs.

Now, here's the catch. This works in both the positive and in the negative. If you're always saying, "I am so unlucky. I never get any good breaks," you're moving toward bad breaks, more disappointment. "Joel, my back has been hurting for three years. I don't think I'll ever get well." You're moving toward more sickness, more pain. "Look, I've been through so much. I don't think I'll ever be happy again." You're moving toward more discouragement, more sadness. If you will change what you're saying, you will change what you're seeing. The Scripture says, "Call the things that are not as if they already were."

A lot of times we do just the opposite. We call the things that are as if they will always be that way. In other words, we just describe the situation. "Gas is so high. I don't see how I'm going to make it." You're calling in more struggle, more lack. "I can't stand my job. My boss gets on my nerves." You're calling in more frustration, more defeat. Don't use your words to describe the situation. Use your words to change the situation.

Have a Better Say So

One time our daughter, Alexandra, had a copy of my first book from ten years ago and a copy of my newest book. She was comparing the photos on the cover. She exclaimed, "Wow, Daddy! You look better today than you did ten years ago." I said, "What would you like me to buy you?"

Do you know how many times I have said, "I'm getting stronger, healthier, wiser. My youth is being renewed like the eagles." Every time you say it, you're moving toward it. But if you're always saying, "I'm so out of shape. I'll never lose this weight," you're moving toward the wrong thing.

A gentleman who looked to be about seventy recently told me, "Joel, when you get old, it's all downhill." That was his *say so*. He was declaring, "I'm going down." He was calling in poor health, lack of vision, and hearing loss. If he keeps that up, he'll keep moving toward it. By the way he looked, he had already been saying it for a long time!

I realize we're all going to get old. We're all eventually going to die, but don't make plans to go downhill. Don't start speaking defeat over your life. Moses was one hundred and twenty years old when he died, and the Scripture says, "His eye was not dim, his natural strength not abated." One hundred and twenty. Healthy. Strong. Twenty-twenty vision. Didn't have reading glasses. Wasn't wearing a "Help! I've fallen and I can't get up" button around his chest! He had a clear memory, a strong, sharp mind. In spite of how you feel, in spite of what's been passed down in your family line, every day you need to declare, "Everything about me is getting better and better—my bones, my joints, my ligaments, my blood, my organs, my memory, my vision, my hearing, my talent, my skill, my looks, my skin. My youth is being renewed. Like Moses, I will finish my course with my eye not dim, my natural strength not abated." You talk like that, and you're moving toward renewed youth, health, energy, and vitality.

That's a lot better than getting up in the morning, looking in the mirror, and saying, "Oh, man, I'm getting so old. Look at these wrinkles. I look so bad. This gray hair. I'm so out of shape." You keep moving toward that, and in five years it's going to be scary! You need to have a better *say so*. Don't talk about the way you are. Talk about the way you want to be. You are prophesying your future.

There's a young lady on staff at Lakewood. Every morning before she leaves her house, she looks in the mirror and says, "Girl, you're looking good today." I saw her one time and asked if she was still doing it. She said, "Yeah, in fact, today when I looked in the mirror, I said, 'Girl, some days you look good; but today, you look *really* good.'"

Why don't you stop criticizing yourself? Stop talking about all the things

> *Why don't you stop criticizing yourself?*

you don't like—how you're getting too old, too wrinkled, too this, too that. Start calling yourself strong, healthy, talented, beautiful, and young. Every morning, before you leave your house, look in the mirror and say, "Good morning, you good-looking thing!"

Turn It Around

Maybe you're in a difficult time today. To complain, "I don't think I'll ever get out," is just going to draw in more defeat. Your declaration should be, "I have grace for this season. I am strong in the Lord. Those who are for me are greater than those who are against me." When you say that, strength comes. Courage comes. Confidence comes. Endurance comes. If you go through a disappointment, a bad break, or a loss, don't grumble, "I don't know why this has happened to me. It's so unfair." That's just going to draw in more self-pity. Your declaration should be, "God promised me beauty for ashes, joy for mourning. I'm not staying here. I'm moving forward. New beginnings are in my future. The rest of my life will be the best of my life." When you talk like that, you're moving toward double for your trouble. You're moving away from self-pity and toward God's goodness in a new way.

One of the best things we can do is take a few minutes every morning and make these positive declarations over our lives. Write down not only your dreams, your goals, and your vision, but make a list of any area you want to improve in, anything you want to see changed. Put that list on your bathroom mirror, somewhere private. Before you leave the house, take a couple of minutes and declare that over your life. If you struggle with your self-esteem, feeling less than, you need to declare every day, "I am confident. I am valuable. I am one of a kind. I have royal blood flowing through my veins. I am wearing a crown of favor. I am a child of the Most High God." You declare that, and you'll go out with your shoulders back, with your head held high.

If you struggle with your weight, declare, "I am in shape. I am healthy. I'm full of energy. I weigh what I should weigh." It may not be true right now, but you keep saying it and you're going to move toward it.

Instead of living under a blanket of guilt and condemnation and being focused on past mistakes, declare, "I am forgiven. I am redeemed. I am wearing a robe of righteousness. God is pleased with me."

> *"Let the weak say, 'I am strong.'"*

The Scripture says, "Let the weak say, 'I am strong.'" It doesn't say, "Let the weak talk about the weakness. Discuss the weakness. Call five friends and explain the weakness." You have to send your words out in the direction you want your life to go.

When you're in a tough time and somebody asks you how you're doing, don't go through a sad song of everything that's wrong in your life. "Oh, man, my back's been hurting. Traffic is so bad today. My boss isn't treating me right. The dishwasher broke. The goldfish died, and my dog doesn't like me." All that's going to do is draw in more defeat. Turn it around. Have a report of victory. "I am blessed.

I am healthy. I am prosperous. I have the favor of God." What you consistently talk about, you're moving toward.

Talk to the Mountain

This is what David did. When he faced Goliath, it looked impossible. All the odds were against him. He could have easily gone around saying, "I know I'm supposed to face Goliath, but look at him. He's twice my size. He's got more experience, more equipment, more talent. I don't see how this is ever going to work out." You can talk yourself out of your destiny. Negative words can keep you from becoming who you were created to be. David looked Goliath in the eyes and said, "You come against me with a sword and a shield. But I come against you in the name of the Lord God of

> *Negative words can keep you from becoming who you were created to be.*

Israel. This day, I will defeat you and feed your head to the birds of the air!" Notice he was prophesying victory. He may have felt fear, but he spoke faith. I can hear David, as he's going out to face Goliath, affirming under his breath, "I am well able. I am anointed. I am equipped. If God be for me, who dare be against me?" He picked up that rock, slung it in his slingshot, and Goliath came tumbling down.

When you face giants in life, you have to do as David did and prophesy your future. "Cancer, you are no match for me. I will defeat you." "This addiction may have been in my family for years, but this is a new day. The buck stops with me. I'm the difference maker. I am free." "My child may have been off course for a long time, but I know it's only temporary. As for me and my house, we will serve the Lord."

There was a man in the Scripture name Zerubbabel. He faced a huge mountain. To rebuild the temple in Jerusalem was a big obstacle, with enemies opposing every step. But like David, he didn't talk about how impossible it was, how it was never going to work out. He said, "Who are you, oh great mountain, that would stand before me? You shall become a mere molehill." He was prophesying his future. The mountain looked big. But he declared it would be flattened out. It would become a molehill. Here's the principle: Don't talk about the mountain; talk to the mountain. Look at that mountain of debt and tell it, "You can't defeat me. You're coming down. I will lend and not borrow. My cup will run over." Whatever mountains you face in life, no matter how big they look, don't shrink back in fear or be intimidated. Rise up in faith and tell that mountain, "You're coming down." Tell that sickness, "You're temporary."

Say to that loneliness, that addiction, that legal problem, "Who are you, oh great mountain, to stand before me?" In other words, "Don't you know who I am? A child of the Most High God. Haven't you read my birth certificate? My Father created the universe. He breathed life into me and crowned me with His favor. He called me more than a conqueror. That means you can't defeat me. You can't hold me back. Oh great mountain, you've got to come down. I will overcome this illness. I will break this addiction. I will pay my house off. I will see my family restored. I will accomplish my dreams."

Prophesy victory. Prophesy breakthroughs. Prophesy what you're believing for.

Resurrect What Looks Dead

In the Old Testament, Ezekiel saw a vision. He had this dream of a valley filled with bones. It was like a huge graveyard. Everywhere he looked were acres and acres of bones from people who had died. Bones represent things in our life that look dead, situations that seem impossible and permanently unchanging. God told him to do something interesting. He said, "Ezekiel, prophesy to these dead bones. Say to them, 'Oh, you dry bones, hear the word of the Lord.'" Ezekiel, in this vision, started speaking to the bones, telling them to come back to life. He called in skin, muscle, and tissue. As he was speaking, the bones started rattling and coming together, just like out of a movie, morphing back into a person. Finally, God told him to "prophesy to the breath" and call it forth. The Scripture says, "As he prophesied, breath came into those bodies, and they stood up like a vast army."

You may have things in your life that seem dead—a relationship, a business, your health. All you can see is a valley of dry bones, so to speak. God is saying to you what He said to Ezekiel. It's not enough to just pray about it; you need to speak to it. Prophesy to those dead bones. Call in health. Call in abundance. Call in restoration. That child who's been off course, don't just pray about him or her. Prophesy and say, "Son, daughter, come back in. You will fulfill your destiny." If you're struggling with an addiction, don't just pray about it, but prophesy. "I am free. Chains are broken off me. This is a new day of victory." Get your checkbook out and prophesy to it. All it looks like are dead bones. Debt. Lack. Struggle. "I prophesy to these dead bones that I will lend and not borrow. I am the head and not the tail. I am coming in to overflow." Just as with Ezekiel, if you'll prophesy to the bones, God will resurrect what looks dead. He'll make things happen that you could never make happen.

A friend of mine smoked cigarettes from an early age. She had tried again and again to stop but couldn't do it. She was constantly saying, "I'll never break this addiction. It's too hard. And if I do, I know I'll gain so much weight." This went on for years. One day

someone told her what I'm telling you, to change what she was saying, to prophesy victory. She started saying, "I don't like to smoke.
I can't stand the taste of nicotine. I'm going to quit and not gain
any extra weight." She said that day after day. Even when she was
smoking and enjoying it, she would say, "I can't stand to smoke."
She wasn't talking about the way she was. She was talking about the
way she wanted to be. About three months later, one morning she
noticed the cigarette tasted funny, almost bitter. She thought she
got a bad pack. It got worse and worse. Several months later, it had
gotten so bad she couldn't stand it anymore. She stopped smoking,
and she never gained one extra pound. Today she is totally free. She
broke that addiction, in part, by the power of her words. She prophesied her future.

Maybe like her, you've spent years saying negative things over
your life. "I can't break this addiction. My marriage is never going to
make it. I'll never get out of debt." You have to send your words out
in a new direction. You are prophesying the wrong thing. Get in a
habit of making these positive declara-
tions over your life. Every day declare
that your dreams are coming to pass.
It's not enough to just believe it. Nothing happens until you speak. As was
true of the psalmist, when you say of the Lord, God will do what
He promised.

> *Every day declare that your dreams are coming to pass.*

Personal "Say So"s

Let me lead you in a few "Say So"s. Make these declarations out
loud.

"I will accomplish my dreams. The right people are in my future.

The right opportunities are headed my way. Blessings are chasing me down."

"I am the head and not the tail. I will lend and not borrow."

"I have a good personality. I am well liked. I am fun to be around. I enjoy my life. I have a positive outlook."

"I will overcome every obstacle. I will outlast every adversity. Things have shifted in my favor. What was meant for my harm, God is using for my advantage. My future is bright."

"My children are mighty in the land. My legacy will live on to inspire future generations."

"I run with purpose in every step. My best days are still out in front of me. My greatest victories are in my future. I will become everything I was created to be. I will have everything God intended for me to have. I am the redeemed of the Lord, and I *say so* today!"

CHAPTER FOUR

A Magnet for Blessings

When you honor God with your life, keeping Him in first place, He puts something on you called *a commanded blessing*. The commanded blessing is like a magnet. It attracts the right people, good breaks, contracts, ideas, resources, and influence. You don't have to go after these things, trying to make something happen in your own strength, your own talent, hoping that life works out. All you have to do is keep honoring God, and the right people will find you. The right opportunities will come across your path. The favor, the wisdom, and the vindication will track you down. Why? You've become a magnet for God's goodness.

The military has what's called a heat-seeking missile. They program a target into the computer and fire the missile off, which can travel thousands of miles. The intended target can be flying in the air, zigzagging here and there, trying to lose it. But it doesn't have a chance. That heat-seeking missile follows it everywhere it goes. It eventually overtakes it and accomplishes its purpose.

In the same way, when you keep God in first place, just like that heat-seeking missile finding a target, God will send blessings that chase you down, favor that overtakes you. Out of nowhere, a good break comes. Suddenly your health improves. Out of the blue, you're able to pay your house off. Unexpectedly, a dream comes to pass. That's not a lucky break. That's not a coincidence. That's the commanded blessing on your life. Like a magnet, you're attracting the goodness of God.

> *Out of nowhere, a good break comes. That's not a coincidence.*

That's what it says in Deuteronomy 28: "When you walk in God's ways, making pleasing Him your highest priority, all these blessings will chase you down and overtake you." One translation says, "You will become a magnet for blessings." That means because you are honoring God, right now, something is attracted to you. Not fear, sickness, depression, or bad breaks. No, like a heat-seeking missile, favor is tracking you down, promotion is headed your way, divine connections are searching you out. You are attracting the goodness of God.

You may be facing an illness. Instead of thinking, *I'm never going to get well. You should see the medical report,* your attitude should be, *Healing is looking for me. Restoration is tracking me down.* If you're struggling in your finances, instead of thinking, *I'll never get out of debt. I'll never accomplish my dreams,* you need to tell yourself, *Abundance is looking for me. Favor is in my future. Good breaks are tracking me down.* If you're single, don't conclude, *I'll never get married. I'm too old. It's been too long.* No, you need to declare, *The right person is looking for me. Divine connections are tracking me down. They're already in my future. Like a magnet, I'm drawing them in.*

Keep Being Your Best

When I look back over my life, it is evident that most of the favor and most of the good breaks came to me. I didn't go after them. I was simply being my best, and God did more than I could ask or think. I never thought I could stand up in front of people and minister. I spent seventeen years behind the scenes at Lakewood doing the television production. I'm not bragging, but during those seventeen years, I was faithful. I gave it my all. I made my father look the best I possibly could. I'd go the extra mile to make sure the lighting was perfect, camera angles were just right. I would even go over to my parents' house every Saturday night and pick out a suit and a tie for my father to wear the next day on television. My mother would say, "Joel, Daddy's a grown man. You don't need to come over every week. He can pick out his own clothes." The problem is, I had seen what my father picked out before! Let's just say he liked a lot of color. I wanted that broadcast to be perfect. I wasn't looking to become Lakewood's senior pastor. I was content where I was behind the scenes. But when my father went to be with the Lord, this opportunity came looking for me. I never planned on doing it; it chased me down.

God's dream for your life is so much bigger than your own. If you will keep being your best right where you are, you will come into favor, promotion, and opportunity bigger than you ever imagined. You won't have to go after it; it will come to you. Like a magnet, you'll draw it in.

> *If you will keep being your best right where you are, you will come into favor, promotion, and opportunity bigger than you ever imagined.*

When I was in my early twenties, I walked into a jewelry store

and met Victoria for the first time. Like a magnet, she couldn't keep
her hands off me! (That's my side of the story anyway.) We went
out on our first date and had so much fun. It was at the Compaq
Center, where we now have our services. The next week she invited
me to come to her house and have dinner. We laughed and had a
great time. I called her the next day at work to thank her, but she
was busy and not able to talk. I called her that evening at home, and
she wasn't there. I called her the next day and the next day and the
next and the next. But she was always either busy or not available;
for some reason she couldn't talk. Finally, I got the message. She's
avoiding me. She doesn't want to see me. I thought, *That's fine. I
won't call her anymore.* About two weeks later, I was sitting in a little
diner eating breakfast early one morning all by myself, and Victoria
came walking in. She saw my car out in the parking lot, came in and
sat at the table, and said, "Joel, I'm so sorry I keep missing all of your
calls." She came back to her senses and came looking for me! (Again,
that's my side of the story. In reality, she ate breakfast and then made
me pay for it.)

Friend, God has the right people in your future. When you honor
God, the person He has designed for you, the right one, will come
across your path as though drawn by a magnet. You don't have to
worry. You don't have to play games and try to convince somebody
to like you. If they don't like you, let them go. If they don't celebrate
you and see you as a gift, a treasure, as one of a kind, move forward.
Don't hang on to people who are not attracted to you. The right
person will not be able to live without you. The one whom God
designed for you will think you're the greatest thing in the world.
You keep being your best right where you are, honoring God, and
God will do for you what He did for me. He'll cause you to be at
the right place at the right time. Those divine connections will come
across your path.

It Will Happen at the Exact Right Time

What God has planned for you is much bigger than anything you've ever dreamed. If God were to show you right now where He's taking you—the favor, the promotion, the influence—it would boggle your mind. You may think, as I did, that you're not the most qualified. You don't have the personality or the talent. That's okay. It's not going to happen just because of your talent, your personality, or your hard work. It's going to happen because of the commanded blessing on your life. God's anointing on you is more important than your talent, your education, or what family you come from. You could have less talent, but with the favor of God, you will go further than people who have much more talent. You may not see how this can happen. It doesn't seem possible. But you don't have to figure it out. If you'll just keep being your best right where you are, getting to work on time, doing more than you have to, being a person of excellence and integrity, the right people will find you and the right opportunities will track you down.

Now, don't be frustrated if it doesn't happen on your timetable. You have to pass some tests. You have to prove to God that you'll be faithful right where you are. If you're not faithful in the wilderness, how can God trust you to be faithful in the Promised Land? You have to keep a good attitude when you're not getting your way. You have to be your best when you're not getting any credit. Do the right thing when it's difficult. That's when your character is being developed. If you pass these tests, you can be certain God will get you to where you're sup-

> *Keep a good attitude when you're not getting your way. Do the right thing when it's difficult.*

posed to be. The right people are in your future. So are the right opportunities, the good breaks, the wisdom, the contracts, the houses. God said, "No good thing will He withhold because you walk uprightly."

I've learned that in a split second one touch of God's favor can take you further than you could go in your whole lifetime on your own. Quit thinking, *I'm getting further behind. I'll never accomplish my dreams.* No; God has explosive blessings in your future. He has blessings that will thrust you years and years ahead.

You say, "Joel, this all sounds good. But I don't really have the talent. I don't know the right people. I don't have the money." That's okay; God does. He's already lined up everything you need. There are good breaks right now that have your name on them. There are contracts, buildings, and businesses that have your name on them. There are ideas, inventions, books, movies, and songs that have your name on them. As you keep honoring God, being your best, like that magnet, you're going to draw in what already has your name on it.

When is this going to happen? At the exact right time. If it hasn't happened yet, don't get discouraged. God knows what He's doing. If it would have happened earlier, it wouldn't have been the best time. Just keep being faithful right where you are and keep living with this attitude that something good is coming your way.

When you do that, you're going to draw in like a magnet what already has your name on it. There's healing with your name on it. If you're single, there's a spouse with your name on him or her. If you're believing to have a child, there's a baby with your name on him or her. God has already chosen them to be yours. There's a business with your name on it. There's a number one movie with your name on it. There's an invention that will touch the world with your name on it.

Your "Eventually"s Will Track You Down

Here's the whole key. You don't have to seek the blessing. Seek God, and the blessings will seek after you. This is where we miss it. Very often, we think, *I have to get this promotion. I have to meet this person. I must get my career going faster.* And yes, we have to use our talents, be determined, and take steps of faith. But you can stay in peace. You can live at rest, knowing that because you're honoring God, the right people will find you. The right opportunities will track you down.

Proverbs says, "The wealth of the ungodly will eventually find its way into the hands of the righteous for whom it has been laid up." Notice that, because you're the righteous, there's something God has laid up for you. The good news is, at the right time, eventually it's going to find you. That means right now, something's looking for you—not defeat, struggle, lack. You are the righteous. Favor is looking for you. Good breaks are looking for you. Healing is looking for you. Influence is looking for you. You may not have seen it yet, but don't get discouraged. Keep honoring God, and He promises some of these "eventually"s are going to track you down.

> *Favor is looking for you. Good breaks are looking for you.*

Our beautiful facility, the former Compaq Center, is an "eventually." It was laid up for us. It had our name on it, and at the right time, it found us. The building was built back in the early 1970s. It was first called the Summit. Then the name was changed to the Compaq Center. But I believe if you'd peeled back the names when it was built way back then, you would have seen the name "Lakewood Church." God had us in mind when it was built. Eventually, God said, "All right, it's time to hand it over."

In the same way, there are some "eventually"s in your future. The great thing is, you don't have to go after them; just go after God. Keep Him in first place. Live a life of excellence and integrity, and God promises the "eventually"s will find their way into your hands. This is what Jesus said: "Seek first the Kingdom and all these things will be added unto you." Everything you need to fulfill your destiny has already been laid up for you. Now

> *Everything you need to fulfill your destiny has already been laid up for you.*

you just have to make pleasing God your highest priority. In other words, before you give in to temptation, be firm and say, "No, I'm going to please God and walk away. I want to fulfill my destiny. I want to come in to my 'eventually's." Before you tell that person off, stop and declare, "No, I'm going to please God and keep my mouth closed." At the office, when they're not treating you right and you feel like slacking off, overcome that attitude and state, "I'm going to please God and keep being my best. I know I'm not working unto people; I'm working unto God." You live like that, and all the forces of darkness cannot keep you from your destiny.

The amazing thing about our church facility is that I didn't go after it; it came to me. Twice, I tried to buy land and build a new sanctuary, but both times, the property was sold out from under us. I thought, *We're stuck. There's no more room. There's no way to grow.* But one day out of the blue, an old friend unexpectedly called and said he wanted to talk to me about something. He said, "Joel, the Houston Rockets basketball team is about to move out of the Compaq Center. That would be a great facility for Lakewood." When he said that, something came alive inside me. I never dreamed we could have something this beautiful or special. It is the premier facility in the fourth-largest city in America, and it is on the second busiest freeway in the nation.

As was true for us, the "eventually"s God has lined up for you are going to boggle your mind. They are going to be more than you can ask or think. God has not only already arranged them; He's taken it one step further. He's already put your name on them. They've already been marked as a part of your divine destiny. What's your part? Worry? Struggle? Try to make it happen? Manipulate this person, and maybe they'll do you a favor? No, you don't have to play up to people. You don't have to beg people, hope that they'll throw you a crumb here or there. You are not a beggar; you are a child of the Most High God. You have royal blood flowing through your veins. You are wearing a crown of favor. The Creator of the universe has called you, equipped you, empowered you, and chosen you.

All you have to do is keep honoring God and the blessings will find you. The right people will show up, the ones who want to help you. The good breaks, the businesses, and the contracts will track you down. One phone call, one person whom God has ordained to help you, can change the course of your life. How is this going to happen? Is it just through your talent, your ability, and your hard work? That's part of it, but the main key is by honoring God. That's what puts you in a position for His blessings to overtake you. That's what makes you a magnet for His favor.

Dream Big. Believe Big. Pray Big.

I know you are a strong, powerful magnet. You are very close to attracting that for which you've been praying and believing. You've honored God. You've been faithful. Now God is about to release an "eventually" in your life. It's going to be bigger than you imagined. When you meet that person, they're going to be better for you than you ever dreamed. You waited a long time, but when they show up, you're going to say, "You were well worth the wait."

"Well, Joel, you're just getting my hopes up." You're right. You can't have faith if you don't first have hope. It's easy to get stuck in a rut, thinking, *God has been good to me. I have a good family. I'm healthy. I'm blessed.* But you haven't seen anything yet. You haven't scratched the surface of what God has in store.

Some of you are going to write a book, a movie, or a song that will touch the world. The idea will come to you. You don't have to go after it. Some of you are going to start a business that will become a global force. Some of you are going to have a ministry that will shake nations. Some of you will raise a child who will become a president or a world leader—a history maker. The "eventually"s God has in your future are going to boggle your mind. It's like nothing you've seen before. God has raised you up to take new ground for the Kingdom, to go where others have not gone.

Dream big. Believe big. Pray big. Make room for God to do something new in your life.

If you would have told me years ago that one day I would be ministering around the world and have books translated into different languages, I would have thought, *Not me. I don't have anything to say.* But God knows what He's put in you—the gifts, the talents, the potential. You have seeds of greatness inside you. Doors are going to open that no man can shut. Talent is going to come out of you that you didn't know you had. God is going to connect you with the right people. He will present you with opportunities that will thrust you into a new level of your destiny.

> *You have seeds of greatness inside you. Doors are going to open that no man can shut.*

When my father was alive, Victoria and I went to India with him a couple of times a year. One time, we met a young pastor who came from an extremely poor family. They didn't have electricity or running water and lived out in an open field in a little hut that they had built. The man next door was very wealthy. He owned a huge farm with thousands of cattle, many different crops, and he sold milk and vegetables to the village people. But he was greedy and charged more than he should have. Many people couldn't afford it.

One day, about ten of the wealthy farmer's cows got out and came over to the little hut where the pastor and his family lived. Having just one cow was a big deal, because it would provide milk and other products to sell to people. The workers came and retrieved those ten cows, then put them back inside the owner's fence. The next day, the same ten cows got out and came back over. This happened again and again and again. The owner got so frustrated, he told his workers, "Just tell the pastor he can have those ten cows." He gave them to him as a gift!

The pastor was thrilled and started selling milk and other dairy products to the people in the village, but he sold the products for much less. Before long, people were lined up at his door. He was able to buy more cows. His business kept growing so much that the owner of the large farm came over and said, "You're putting me out of business. I can't compete with you. Why don't you take over my company?" The pastor purchased his company for a fraction of its value, and today he has a very successful company with several hundred employees. But it all started when the cows came looking for him and wouldn't go home. What is that? Like a magnet, he attracted the goodness of God.

You don't have to worry about how it's all going to work out. God knows how to have the cows find you. What has your name on it—the real estate, the good breaks, the businesses, the favor—will eventually find its way into your hands. Proverbs says it this way: "Trouble chases sinners, while blessings chase the righteous!" You are the righteous. Right now, favor is chasing you. Promotion is chasing you. Healing is chasing you. Cows might be looking for you! Victory is coming your way.

Turn Up the Power

Don't ever say, "I'll never get out of debt." "I'll never get married." "I'll never be well again." Do you know what that's doing? Demagnetizing your magnet. It's taking away the attraction power.

When I was a little boy, I used to play with a magnet. One day, I discovered the magnet had lost its drawing power. I had left it by something that demagnetized it. It looked the same, but it wouldn't attract anything. In the same way, when we dwell on negative thoughts—can't do it, not able to, never going to happen—that is demagnetizing our magnet. You are taking away its power to pull in what belongs to you.

Do you know what I'm doing today? I'm helping you to turn up the power on your magnet. When you realize God has put a commanded blessing on your life, and you go out each day with the attitude that something good is going to happen to you, that's when God can do the exceedingly, abundantly, above and beyond.

> *Go out each day with the attitude that something good is going to happen to you.*

Each of us can look back over our life and remember a time when we unexpectedly saw God's favor. You didn't go after it; it came after you. God has done it in the past, and the good news is He's not only going to do it again in the future, but what He's going to show you will make what you've seen pale in comparison. He has explosive blessings coming your way. They are going to thrust you to a level greater than you've imagined. You're going to look back and join me in saying, "How in the world did I get here? I'm not the most qualified or the most talented. I don't have all the experience." You may not, but God does. He knows how to get you to where you're supposed to be. All through the day, make this declaration: "I am blessed."

I believe today the power of your magnet is being turned up. You're about to draw in good breaks, promotion, healing, favor, ideas, contracts, and creativity. God is about to release what already has your name on it. You're not going to have to go after it; it's going to come after you. It's going to be bigger than you imagined. It's going to happen sooner than you thought. You're about to step into the fullness of your destiny and become everything God has created you to be.

I AM
FREE

CHAPTER FIVE

Your Seventh Year

When we've struggled in an area for a long time, it's easy to think, *This is the way it's always going to be. I'll always struggle in my finances. I never get any good breaks. My marriage will never improve. We just don't get along.* Too often we see it as permanent. People tell me, "I've always been negative. That's just who I am." They've convinced themselves that it's never going to change.

The first place we lose the battle is in our own thinking. If you think it's permanent, then it's permanent. If you think you've reached your limits, you have. If you think you'll never get well, you won't. You have to change your thinking. You need to see everything that's holding you back—every limitation, every

> *The first place we lose the battle is in our own thinking.*

addiction, every sickness—as only temporary. It didn't come to stay; it came to pass. The moment you accept it as the norm, the moment you decide, *This is my lot in life*, that's when it can take root and become a reality. A stronghold in your mind can keep you from your destiny. If you would just break out in your thinking, you would see things begin to improve.

You may have struggled in an area for twenty years. The medical report says, "Just learn to live with it." But there is another report. It says, "God is restoring health back unto you. The number of your days He will fulfill." Your attitude should be, *This sickness cannot stay in my body. It's on foreign territory. I am a temple of the Most High God.* In your career you may feel stuck. You haven't had a good break in a long time. You've gone as far as your education allows. It's easy to think, *I've reached my limits. This is as good as it gets.* All through the day you should declare, "I'm not settling here. My greatest victories are still out in front of me."

You have to stir up your faith. God is not limited by your education, by your nationality, or by your background. But He is limited by your thinking. I'm asking you to stand against the lies of permanency, lies that state, "You'll never lose that weight. You'll never break that addiction. You'll never own your own house." When those thoughts come, dismiss them. Don't give them the time of day. God is saying, "It's not permanent; it's temporary. It didn't come to stay; it came to pass."

The Seventh Year

In Deuteronomy 15, there was a law God gave the people of Israel that said every seventh year they had to release any Hebrew slaves. If you were Hebrew and owed another person money that you couldn't repay, they could take you in as a slave and make you work full-time until you paid them back. But every seventh year, if you were a part of God's chosen people, you had a special advantage. You got released. No matter how much you still owed, no matter how in debt you were, in the seventh year you were set free. All the pain, struggling, and suffering were gone in one day. This tells me God never intended His people to be a permanent slave to anything. You may be in debt today, but God did not intend that to last forever. You may be facing an illness, but it is only temporary. You may be struggling with an addiction, but it's not going to keep you in bondage.

I believe you are coming into one of your seventh years. The seventh year is when you break free from any limitation that is holding you back—sickness, addictions, debt, constant struggles. It looked as though it would never change.

> *The seventh year is when you break free from any limitation that is holding you back—sickness, addictions, debt, constant struggles.*

It looked permanent, but then one touch of God's favor and it suddenly turns around. Suddenly you get a good break. Suddenly your health improves. Suddenly you meet the right person. Suddenly a dream comes to pass. What happened? You came into a seventh year.

Quit telling yourself, "This sickness is permanent. I'll always struggle financially. I'll never break this addiction." You are a child of the Most High God. You have an advantage. Just like God promised the Hebrews, you're not going to be a permanent slave to anything. Now you have to get in agreement with God and affirm, "Yes, I'm coming into my seventh year. It is my time to break free. Every chain has been loosed. Every stronghold has come down. I know I have been released into increase."

I talked to a gentleman in the lobby of our church. He was in town for a consultation at MD Anderson, Houston's world-renowned cancer hospital. For the last three years he had a large tumor in his stomach area. He went through chemotherapy and radiation, but nothing affected it. The doctors had been studying him, trying to figure out what to do next. About six months ago, he came to a Lakewood service for the first time and had one of the volunteer Prayer Partners pray over him. He went back to the hospital for more tests. The doctor was very puzzled. For no apparent reason, the tumor had started to shrink. It was about half of its original size. The man had not had any treatment in a couple of years. The doctor didn't understand it. He asked him, "What have you been doing differently?"

The man replied, "The only thing I've done differently is I've had some people pray over me."

The doctor told him, "You tell those people to keep praying, because at this pace it's going to be totally gone in a few months' time!"

What was that? A seventh year. It looked permanent. Chemotherapy couldn't stop it. Radiation couldn't contain it. But our God can do what medicine cannot do. He is not limited to the natural. He is a supernatural God. It doesn't matter how long it's been that way or how impossible it looks. When you come into your seventh year, all the forces of darkness cannot stop what God wants to do.

You Need to Get Ready

Is there something in your life you think is permanent? You think you'll never get well, never start that business, never settle that legal problem. As far as you can see, your problem is permanent. God is saying, "Get ready. You are coming into your seventh year." The seventh year is a year of release from sickness, disease, and chronic pain. Release from depression, worry, and anxiety. Release from bad habits, from addictions. It's not only a release from limitations; it's a release into increase. God is about to release you into new opportunities, good breaks, and new levels. He is going to release ideas, creativity, sales, contracts, and business. The seventh year is when you get released into overflow, into more than enough. It's when dreams come to pass.

Now, you have to receive this into your spirit today. It's easy to think, *This is never going to happen to me. I don't believe anything is going to change. I don't believe I'm coming into my seventh year.* Then this not for you, because this is for believers. This is for people who know things have shifted in their favor. It is for people who know every limitation is only temporary, for people who know they're entering into their seventh year.

In 2003, Lakewood signed a sixty-year lease with the City of Houston for our facility, the former Compaq Center, where the Rockets used to play basketball. We always wanted to own the facility, but the lease was the best thing at the time. Seven years later, in 2010, the city was running low on tax revenue and decided to sell off some of their properties. They called and asked if we would be interested in purchasing the facility, and of course we were, but it depended on the price. Brand-new, a facility like ours would cost four hundred million dollars. The city ran its own independent appraisal. They got back with us and said, "We will sell it to you, not for four hundred million dollars, not for two hundred million dollars, not for fifty million dollars, but for seven and a half million dollars!" Now we no longer lease. We own the property.

Isn't this interesting? Our seventh year for seven and a half million dollars. Only God can do that. Friend, there are some seventh years in your future! You may think, *I could never afford that property. I could never get well. The chemotherapy didn't work. I'll never meet the right person.* No; you need to get ready. When you come into your seventh year, God is going to do more than you can ask or think. He is going to exceed your expectations. It's going to be bigger, better,

> *It's going to be bigger, better, and more rewarding than you thought possible.*

and more rewarding than you thought possible. It may seem permanent now, but when you come into the seventh year, God is going to release you from leasing into owning. He'll release you from debt into abundance, from sickness into health, from constantly struggling into an anointing of ease. Why don't you get up in the morning and dare to say, "God, I want to thank You that I'm coming into my seventh year. Thank You that You are releasing me into the fullness of my destiny. I am free!" When you believe, all things are possible.

God Can Turn Any Situation Around

I received a letter from a lady who had been in an automobile accident and broken her neck. She lived in constant pain and had had several surgeries. For months her husband had stayed home to take care of her. She felt bad that he had missed so much work, and finally convinced him she was well enough to stay home alone. One day she was in so much pain and so deep in depression that she decided she was going to end her life. She couldn't walk on her own, so she was going to crawl over to the corner where the gun rack was. Her husband was an avid hunter and had several firearms. But when she got out of her chair, she lost her balance, knocked over the end table, fell flat on her back, and couldn't move. The remote control for the television hit the floor, and the batteries tumbled out. When it hit, it changed the channel on the television from what she was watching to a channel where I was speaking. Her first thought was, *Oh, great! I'm lying here dying. Now I've got to listen to this TV preacher to add to my misery.*

That day I was talking about how God can turn any situation around, how He can take your darkest hour and turn it into your brightest hour. She began to feel a peace that she had never felt before. She said, "I was lying there. I couldn't move, couldn't open my eyes, but I felt tears of joy running down my cheeks." Her husband came home a few hours later and found her sound asleep there on the floor. Startled and alarmed, he woke her up saying, "Honey, are you okay? It looks like you've had an accident."

She smiled and said, "It was no accident."

That day was a turning point in her life. Hope began to fill her heart. A dream came back to life. Today, she is not only free from pain but she can walk; she's healthy, whole, and stronger than ever before.

When it looked impossible, when all the odds were against her, when it seemed permanent, the Creator of the universe, the One who has you in the palm of His hand, said, "Wait a minute! She's My child. She's My daughter. She has a special advantage. She is not going to be a permanent slave to anything. She is coming into her seventh year."

Maybe like her, you've lived with that sickness, that chronic pain, long enough. You've put up with that depression, that dark cloud following you around long enough. You've struggled with the addiction long enough. God is saying, "This is your time. Today is your moment. Get ready for release. Get ready for a breakthrough. Get ready for healing. Get ready for increase. Get ready for your seventh year."

> "This is your time. Today is your moment. Get ready for release."

How do you get ready? Start talking as if it's going to happen. Start acting as if it's going to happen. Start thinking as if it's going to happen.

"Well, Joel, my arthritis has really been acting up. My diabetes is getting the best of me. My financial difficulties are really weighing me down." Don't take ownership of those things. It's not your diabetes. It doesn't belong to you. It's not your arthritis. That's not a part of who you are. It may be there temporarily, but that's not where it's staying. Don't give it a permanent address. In your mind, don't let it move in and take up residency. You need to hang one of those signs out that says, NO VACANCY HERE.

The Apostle Paul put it this way: "These light afflictions are for a moment." In your mind, it may be big, but by faith you need to see it as being light and temporary. This is what Moses did. The Israelites had been in slavery for many years. It looked permanent, as though it would never change. Moses had a son, whom he named Gershom. Names had a lot more significance back in those days than they do today. *Gershom* means "I am an alien in a strange land." When Moses named his son, he was making a declaration of faith. He was saying, "We're in slavery, but slavery is not our norm. This is not our permanent address. We are foreigners in this land." Every time he said, "Good morning, Gershom," he was reminding himself, "This lack, this trouble, this slavery, is not our normal state."

When you're in tough times, and it looks as though you're never going to break out, you have to do as Moses did. Tell yourself, "I won't be staying here long. I am a foreigner. I don't have citizenship here." You could say, "I am not a citizen of depression. I'm not a citizen of lack. I'm not a citizen of cancer. This disease is alien to me. It's not my norm. It may be where I am, but it is not who I am. I am blessed. I am healthy. I am strong. I am victorious." Anything to the contrary you need to see as foreign, as temporary. It is not your permanent address.

When You Believe It, You
Will Receive It

In the Scripture, King Hezekiah was very sick. The prophet Isaiah came to visit him at the palace and said, "I have a word from the Lord for you."

I can imagine Hezekiah perked up and replied, "Yes, what is it?"

Isaiah said, "The word is, 'Set your house in order. You will surely die.'"

Not the word he was looking for! I'm sure Hezekiah thought, *Is there another prophet out there?* His situation looked permanent, as though his days were over. The prophet who spoke for God had just announced that Hezekiah's life was coming to an end. Hezekiah could have accepted this and thought, *This is my lot in life.* But he had a boldness. He chose to believe even when things looked impossible. The Scripture says, "He turned his face to the wall and started praying."

"God, I'm asking You to give me more years. God, I'm not finished. I've served You. My family has honored You. God, let me live longer." Before Isaiah could leave the palace grounds, God spoke to him and said, "Go back and tell Hezekiah that I'm going to give him fifteen more years." Here's what I want you to see. Hezekiah's faith is what brought about his seventh year. Your faith is what causes God to move.

"Well, Joel, I'm sixty-five years old, and I've never had a seventh year." Are you releasing your faith? Are you thanking God that it's turning around? Are you declaring, "Where I am is not where I'm staying? This sickness is temporary. I'm coming out of debt. There are new levels in my future. I am free." When you have this attitude of faith, speaking victory over your life, that's when the Creator

> *Your faith can bring about your seventh year.*

of the universe will show up and do amazing things. Your faith can bring about your seventh year.

What's interesting is that when Hezekiah got the news that his life would be extended, he didn't feel any better. He didn't look any different. The only thing that had changed was God had said that his life would be extended. Here's the key: Hezekiah didn't wait for his health to turn around before he gave God praise. He didn't wait until he felt better to start talking as though he were going to live and thinking as though he were well. It's easy to think, *When I see it, I'll believe it*. But faith says, "You have to believe it, and then you'll see it."

Like Isaiah, I've announced to you that you're coming into your seventh year. Now you can look at the circumstances, study the financial report, see how you feel, and think, *It doesn't look any different. I don't see a sign of anything changing. As soon as it starts to improve, I'll give God praise.*

Your praise is what activates God's favor. When you have the boldness of Hezekiah and say, "God, I don't see how I could get well. The medical report doesn't look good. I don't see how I could meet the right person, how I'll ever afford my own home, but God, I believe You have already made a way. I believe I'm stepping into a new season of favor. I believe I'm entering into my seventh year, that every limitation has been broken. So Lord, I just want to thank You for Your goodness in my life."

When you talk as though it's going to happen, act as though it's going to happen, and praise as though it's going to happen, that's when God says to the angels, "Turn around and go back and tell them they're coming into their seventh year. I'm going to do what they're asking. I'm going to change what looked permanent."

But a lot of times instead of taking our praise to God, we're taking our problems to Him. "God, I've had this addiction for twenty-seven years. I don't think I'll ever break it. God, these children are getting on my nerves. You'd better keep me sane. I'm working two jobs and still don't have enough. God, I don't understand it." It's easy to turn prayer into a complaining session, but remember, God already knows your needs. You don't have to tell God everything that's wrong, what you don't like, and how long it's been that way. It's much better to take your praise to God rather than your problems. Your financial situation may not look good, but turn it around. "Lord, I want to thank You that You are supplying all of my needs. Thank You that You are the Lord my Provider." You may not feel well, but instead of complaining, say, "Lord, thank You that I'm getting healthier, stronger, better every day." Your son or daughter isn't doing right. "Lord, thank You that my children will fulfill their destinies." Praise gets God's attention, not complaining.

The Year of God's Favor

When Saul of Tarsus was blinded by that great light on the road to Damascus, God spoke to Ananias to go pray for him. Saul had been killing believers and putting them in prison. Ananias said in Acts 9, "Lord, I have heard many reports about this man, and all the harm that he has done." Notice this passage: "I've heard that he is killing people. I've heard that he is dangerous. I've heard that he doesn't like believers." If you're always telling God what you've heard, you're going to miss out on God's blessings. You'll get discouraged. Doubt will fill your mind. "God, the financial report says I'm never going to get ahead. God, my children are running with the wrong crowd." Here's a key: Don't tell God what you've heard. God says you're the head and not the tail. Now, don't tell Him all the reasons why you're not. God says you will live and not die. "But God, the medical report says otherwise." No; quit telling God what you've heard. That's not doing you or Him any good. It's really simple. Don't take your problems to God; take your praise to God. "Lord, I want to thank You that with long life You will satisfy me. And even though my condition looks permanent, Lord, I want to thank You that I'm coming into my seventh year, a year of release, a year of healing, a year of breakthroughs, a year of abundance."

> *This is a year of release, a year of healing, a year of breakthroughs, a year of abundance.*

Isaiah said, "The Spirit of the Lord is upon me to announce freedom to the captives." He was saying in effect, "Things may look permanent, but I'm announcing your freedom. I'm announcing you're coming out of debt. I'm announcing that sickness is not going to defeat you. I'm announcing new levels are in your future." Then he took it one step further. He said, "I'm declaring the Year of God's Favor." Notice this principle. He announced it, then he declared it.

What if we were to do the same thing? "I'm announcing today we're coming out of debt, struggle, and always being behind. I'm declaring we're coming into increase, overflow, and abundance. I'm declaring we will lend and not borrow. We will be able to give to every good work. I'm declaring we're blessed, prosperous, and generous." Over our families we'd say, "I'm announcing that our children will not run with the wrong crowd, make poor choices, or get into trouble. I'm declaring, 'As for me and my house we will serve the Lord.' I'm declaring, 'The seed of the righteous will be mighty in the land.'" Or how about this? "I'm announcing, 'We will not live negative, depressed, worried, anxious, or stressed-out lives.' I'm declaring, 'We are happy, content, confident, secure, full of joy, and loving our lives.'" You have to announce it and declare it by faith.

Nothing you're saying may be true at the time. This is what faith is all about. Too often we're announcing and declaring the wrong things. "I've been single so long. I'll never meet the right person. Prices are so high. I don't see how I'm ever going to make it." That's announcing defeat and declaring mediocrity. You have to change what's coming out of your mouth. Start announcing freedom from anything that is holding you back. Freedom from loneliness. Freedom from depression. Freedom from addictions. Freedom from constantly struggling.

> *Start announcing freedom from anything that is holding you back.*

Dare to do as Hezekiah did and start boldly declaring, "I am free. I am healthy. I am blessed. I am victorious. God's favor is coming—breakthroughs, healing, and promotion are on the way." You may have struggled in an area for a long time, but let me declare this over you: "It is not permanent. You are coming into your seventh year. This is a new day. The tide of the battle has turned. Every chain has been loosed. Every stronghold has been shattered. Every limitation has been broken. You are breaking free into a new level. I believe and declare God is releasing you into increase. He is releasing you into opportunity, into favor; releasing you into healing, into breakthroughs. He is releasing you into the fullness of your destiny."

I AM
VALUABLE

CHAPTER SIX

Know Who You Are

I grew up watching Archie Manning play football. He was a tremendous NFL quarterback and incredibly talented. Now two of his sons, Peyton and Eli, are both great quarterbacks as well. How could that be? Out of the millions of young men who play football, how can these two stand out? It's not a coincidence. It's in their blood. They have their father's DNA.

When God created you in His image, He put a part of Himself in you. You could say that you have the DNA of Almighty God. You are destined to do great things, destined to leave your mark on this generation. Your Heavenly Father spoke worlds into existence. He flung stars into space. He painted every sunrise. He designed every flower. He made

> *You are destined to do great things, destined to leave your mark on this generation.*

man out of dust and breathed life into him. Now, here's the key: He is not just the Creator of the universe. He is not just the all-powerful God. He is your Heavenly Father. You have His DNA. Imagine what you can do.

But too many times we don't realize who we are. We focus on

our weaknesses, what we don't have, the mistakes we've made, and the family we come from. We end up settling for mediocrity when we were created for greatness. If you're going to break out of average, you need to remind yourself, "I have the DNA of the Most High God. Greatness is in my genes. I come from a bloodline of champions."

When you realize who you are, you won't go around intimidated and insecure, thinking, *I'm lacking. I'm not that talented. I come from the wrong family.* No; you come from the right family. Your Father created it all. When you know who you are, it changes your thinking from, *I'm unlucky. I never get any good breaks,* to *I have the favor of God. Blessings are chasing me down.* From saying, "This obstacle is too big. I'll never overcome it," to declaring, "I can do all things through Christ. If God be for me, who dare be against me?" From looking at your test score and concluding, *I'm an average student. All I can make are C's,* to *I'm an A student. I have the mind of Christ.* From looking in the mirror and thinking, *I don't have a good personality. I'm not that attractive,* to saying, "I am fearfully and wonderfully made. I am one of a kind." When you know who you are, you'll start thinking like a winner, talking like a winner, and carrying yourself like you are a winner.

Who Is Your Father?

I remember a billboard that asked the question, "Who's the father?" It was an advertisement for DNA testing. They can take a child's DNA and test another person's DNA and see if it matches. A match proves the two people are scientifically related. Out of the billions of people on Earth, the chances of your DNA matching someone who's not your family is so small that it's inconceivable. In a similar way, when you gave your life to Christ, the Scripture talks about how you became a new creation. You were born into a new family. You entered into a new bloodline. Now imagine that somehow we could do spiritual DNA testing. They take a sample of DNA from your Heavenly Father, then a sample of DNA from you, and run all the tests. The good news is that it would come back a perfect match. It would prove beyond all doubt that you are God's child. You have His DNA. You come from a royal bloodline.

Given your DNA, don't you dare go around thinking that you're average. *I could never accomplish my dreams. I'll never get out of debt.* Are you kidding? Do you know who your Father is? You have His DNA. He created worlds. There's nothing too much for you. You can overcome that sickness. You can run that company. You can build and support that orphanage. You can take your family to a new level. Quit believing the lies that say, "You've reached your limits. You've gone as far as you can go." Start talking to yourself as a winner. It's in your blood. You're expected to succeed. You're expected to get well. You're expected to live debt free. Why? Because of who your Father is.

In one sense, it's no big deal that I am the pastor of Lakewood Church. My father was a minister for more than fifty years. This is all I had seen growing up. It's in my genes. And it's no big deal to see Archie Manning's sons play professional football. Archie was an NFL Pro Bowl quarterback. In the same way, it's no big deal for you to accomplish your dreams. It's no big deal for you to live healthy and whole. It's no big deal for you to lead the company in sales. Why? Like Father, like son. It's in your spiritual DNA.

I saw a documentary on championship racehorses, the kind you see running in the Kentucky Derby. It's not a coincidence that those horses become the fastest horses in the world. They've been carefully studied and carefully bred for generations. It can cost hundreds of thousands of dollars to breed a racehorse with a champion stallion. Before breeding, the owners will go back fifty or sixty years and study the bloodline of a particular stallion. They'll research his father and grandfather and study how long their strides were, how tall their legs were, their takeoff speed, their endurance. With all this information, they'll choose what they believe to be the perfect match. They understand winners don't just randomly happen.

> *Winners don't just randomly happen. Winning is in their DNA.*

Winning is in their DNA. That's what sets these horses apart. They have generation after generation of champions inside.

When the little colt is born, his legs may be wobbly and he can barely stand up. He doesn't look different from any other colt that is born. The owners could think, *Oh, man. We have wasted our money. This colt is not a thoroughbred. Look at him wobble.* But they're not concerned with his present weaknesses. They're not worried about what color he is, how pretty he is, or even how muscular he is. They are totally confident, knowing that inside that little colt is the DNA of a champion.

It's in Your DNA

That's how it is with you and me. You didn't come from ordinary stock. You came from the best of the best. It doesn't matter what you look like, what color you are, how tall or short, how attractive or unattractive. It doesn't matter how many weaknesses you have. You may struggle with an addiction. You may have made some mistakes. What supersedes all of that is that inside you is the DNA of a champion. You come from a long list of winners.

If you look back and study your spiritual bloodline, you'll see your elder brother defeated the enemy. There's victory in your bloodline. You'll see your ancestor Moses parted the Red Sea. There's great faith in your bloodline. David, a shepherd boy, defeated a giant. There's favor in your bloodline. Samson pushed down the walls of a huge building. There's supernatural strength and power in your bloodline. Nehemiah rebuilt the walls of Jerusalem when all the · odds were against him. There's increase, promotion, and abundance in your bloodline. A young lady named Esther stepped up and saved her people from a certain death. There is courage in your bloodline.

Now, don't go around thinking, *I could never break this addiction. I could never afford college. I'll never see my family restored.* You come from a bloodline of champions. It's in your DNA. You were born to win, born to overcome, born to live in victory. It doesn't matter what your present circumstances look like. That addiction didn't come to stay. Freedom is in your DNA. That sickness is not permanent. Health and wholeness are in your DNA. That family problem, strife, division; they're not going to last forever. Restoration is in your DNA. Lack, struggle, and barely getting by are not your destiny. Abundance, increase, opportunity, and good breaks are in your DNA.

Now, when thoughts tell you that it's never going to happen, just go back and check your spiritual birth certificate. Remind yourself of who you are. When thoughts intrude—*You'll never accomplish your dreams. You'll never get well*—just reply, "No, thanks. You have the wrong person. I've already checked my birth certificate. I know who I am. Now, let me verify what's in my DNA. It's found in God's Word. Am I supposed to live average, lonely, struggling, and always getting the short end of the stick? No; it says in the Psalms, 'God's favor surrounds me like a shield.' It declares, 'No weapon formed against me will prosper.' It says, 'The number of my days He will fulfill.' It states, 'As for me and my house we will serve the Lord.' It says, 'I will lend and not borrow. Goodness and mercy are following us. Good breaks are chasing us down.'" That's what's in your DNA. When thoughts tell you otherwise, don't get discouraged. Just keep checking your spiritual birth certificate. Keep reminding yourself of who you are.

My brother, Paul, and his beautiful wife, Jennifer, have a son named Jackson. When Jackson was a little boy, every night when Jennifer would put him to bed and after she prayed with him, she would go through a long list of superheroes, telling Jackson who he was. That was her way of speaking faith into him, letting him know he was going to do great things. She would say, "All right, Jackson, let me remind you of who you are. You're my Superman. You're my Buzz Lightyear. You're my Power Ranger. You're my Rescue Hero. You're my Lightning McQueen," and on and on. Little Jackson would lie there, a big smile on his face, taking it all in. One night they got home late, and she wasn't able to go through that same routine. She put him to bed in a hurry.

> *"Momma, you forgot to tell me who I am."*

A few minutes later she heard this little voice hollering from his room, "Momma! Momma!" She rushed in and asked, "Jackson, what's wrong?" He said, "Momma, you forgot to tell me who I am."

The Power of the Bloodline

A lot of people in life have never been told who they are. They've had negative voices playing over and over. "You're not talented. You're not going to ever get married. You'll never get out of debt. You've come from the wrong family." As long as those voices are playing, it will keep you from your destiny.

Maybe nobody told you who you are. Let me help you out. Almighty God says:

You're a child of the Most High God.

You are strong. You are talented.

You are beautiful. You are wise.

You are courageous. You have seeds of greatness.

You can do all things through Christ.

You didn't come from ordinary stock.

You're a thoroughbred. You have winning in your DNA.

You are destined to do great things.

In the Old Testament, people understood the power of the bloodline more than we do today. God started the first covenant with a Jewish man named Abraham. Back in those days, if you weren't Jewish, you didn't have a right to God's blessings and favor. It was limited to one bloodline—the Jewish people. In Luke 13, Jesus saw a woman who had been bent over with a sickness for eighteen years. He made an interesting statement. He said, "Should not this woman be loosed from this sickness seeing that she is a daughter of Abraham?" He was saying, "She comes from the right family. Healing is in her DNA. She has a right to be well." Jesus went over and made her whole.

On another occasion, just the opposite happened. A Gentile woman came up and begged Jesus to heal her daughter. Jesus said in effect, "I can't do it. You come from the wrong family." It didn't seem fair, but that's how powerful the bloodline was. In this case, though, despite her Gentile bloodline, Jesus marveled at the woman's faith and eventually healed the daughter.

Here's the beauty. When Jesus died and rose again, He made a way for all people to come to Him, both Jews and Gentiles. Galatians says, "If you're in Christ, you are the seed of Abraham and heirs according to the promise." Don't go through life believing the lies that you've come from the wrong family. "Your mother was depressed. You'll always be depressed." "Your dad was an alcoholic. You'll be an alcoholic." You have entered into a new bloodline. If God was standing before you today, He would say the same thing He said to that first lady. "Should not this man be free from this addiction, seeing that he is a son of Abraham?" "Should not this woman be healthy and whole, seeing that she is a daughter of Abraham?"

Friend, you have a right to be blessed, to be free, to be healthy, to be happy, and to be whole. It's in your DNA. Your natural bloodline may have some negative things in it, but the spiritual bloodline will always overpower your natural bloodline. The spiritual is greater than the natural.

> *Friend, you have a right to be blessed, to be free, to be healthy, to be happy, and to be whole.*

You may think, *I've got a lot of dysfunction in my family. I've got a lot going against me.* But your spiritual bloodline says you can overcome every obstacle. You can break that addiction. You can beat that sickness. You can take your family to a new level. Why? You come from the right bloodline. You have the DNA of a champion.

You Are a Mighty Hero

In Judges 6, the Midianites had overtaken the people of Israel. They were making their lives miserable. When the Israelites' crops came up, the Midianites would go in and destroy the produce. They were a bigger and stronger nation. It looked as though they would eventually drive the Israelites away. There was a man named Gideon who was hiding in the fields, afraid of the Midianites. An angel appeared to him and said, "Mighty hero, the Lord is with you."

I can imagine Gideon looked around and thought, *Who's he talking about? I'm not a mighty hero.* Gideon wasn't strong and courageous. He was just the opposite; afraid and intimidated, yet God called him a mighty hero. Like Gideon, you may feel weak, but God calls you strong. You may feel intimidated; God calls you courageous. You may feel inadequate; God calls you well able. You may think you're average, but God calls you a mighty hero. When you get up in the morning and the negative thoughts come, reminding you of what you're not, telling you of all your flaws and weaknesses, put your shoulders back, hold your head up high, dare to look in the mirror, and say, "Good morning, you mighty hero." Let these thoughts play all through the day. "I am strong. I am courageous. I have the DNA of a champion. I am who God says I am. I can do what God says I can do." You have to remind yourself of who you truly are. You are a mighty hero.

The angel went on to say, "Gideon, you are to deliver God's people from the Midianites."

Gideon said, "How can I do that? I come from the poorest family. I am the least one in my father's house."

What was the problem? Gideon didn't know who he was. God had just called him a mighty hero. A couple of chapters later, Gideon was interrogating his enemies. He asked them, "What did the men look like whom you saw?"

They said, "Gideon, they looked like you, like a king's son."

Here, Gideon had felt as though he was the least, inadequate, and not able to. But even his enemies said, "You look like a king's son."

If you allow the wrong thoughts to play in your mind, you can have the talent, the opportunity, the strength, and the looks, but like

Gideon you'll make excuses and talk yourself out of it. I love the fact that God not only calls you a mighty hero but even the enemy sees

> *God not only calls you a mighty hero but even the enemy sees you as a king's son, a king's daughter.*

you as a king's son, a king's daughter. He knows who you are. Now, make sure you know who you are. Carry yourself like a king, like a queen, like a mighty hero. You come from the right family.

It's interesting, when God called Gideon a mighty hero, up to that point Gideon had not done anything significant. He had not parted a Red Sea as Moses had. He had not defeated a giant as David did. He had not brought somebody back to life as the prophet Elijah had. I can understand God calling him a mighty hero if he had done something amazing. But it seemed that there was nothing special about him—just an ordinary, insignificant man. But God saw something in Gideon that other people did not see: God saw his potential. God saw what he could become.

You may feel that you're average. You may think you're ordinary, but God sees the mighty hero in you. God sees the DNA of a champion. He sees the king's son, the king's daughter. Now, do yourself a favor. Turn off the negative recording that's reminding you of what you're not, and get in agreement with God. Start seeing yourself as that mighty hero.

When God told Moses to go speak to Pharaoh and tell him to let the people go, the first thing Moses said was, "Who am I?" He was saying, "God, I'm ordinary. Pharaoh is the leader of a nation. He is not going to listen to me." Moses forgot who he was. He didn't see himself as a king's son but as inadequate. He focused on his weaknesses, his limitations. He started making excuses. He said, "God, I can't go talk to Pharaoh. I stutter. I've got a problem with my speech."

God said, "Moses, who made your tongue? Who makes the deaf to hear? Who makes the blind to see?" God was saying, "Moses, I breathed My life into you. I put My DNA inside you. You may feel weak, inadequate, and insecure, but Moses, I don't want to hear your excuses. Quit telling Me what you're not. I have the final say, and I say you're a king's son. I say you're a mighty hero." That's what God is saying to each one of us today.

Have an Eagle Mentality

I heard a story about an eagle that was born in a chicken coop and raised with a brood of chickens. For years he pecked like a chicken, bawked like a chicken, and ate like a chicken. That's all he had ever seen. But one day he looked up and saw an eagle soaring in the sky. Something deep inside said, "That's what you were created to do." His DNA was calling out to him. But when he looked around, all of his circumstances said, "You're just a chicken."

He got his courage up. He told his chicken buddies that he was going to soar like that eagle. They laughed at him and said, "Are you kidding? You can't soar. You're just a chicken."

All he had ever heard was *chicken*. *Chicken* had become ingrained in his thinking, but deep down something said, "This is not who I am. I wasn't made to be average, to live in this limited environment. I may be in a chicken coop, but I don't feel like a chicken. I don't think like a chicken. I don't look like a chicken. This is not my destiny. I have the DNA of an eagle."

He started noticing that his wings were not like the chickens'. His were bigger, stronger, and wider. He decided to try to fly. Flapping his wings back and forth as fast as he could, the eagle barely lifted off the ground and crashed into the side of the chicken coop. His chicken friends laughed and said, "We told you. You're no different from us. You're wasting your time. You're a chicken." He didn't let that failure, nor what the others said, nor the disappointment talk him out of it. Every day he kept trying, being his best. One day he

With every breath he declared, "This is what I was created for. This is who I really am. I knew I was an eagle!"

lifted up out of that chicken coop and began to soar up and up in the sky. With every breath he declared, "This is what I was created for. This is who I really am. I knew I was an eagle!"

Perhaps you've been in a chicken coop way too long. Let me tell you what you already know. You're not a chicken. You're an eagle. Don't let that limited environment rub off on you. Don't let how you were raised or what somebody said keep you from knowing who you really are. Check your spiritual birth certificate. You'll find you've been made in the image of Almighty God. He has crowned you with favor. You have royal blood flowing through your veins. You were never created to be average or mediocre. You were created to soar. Abundance, opportunity, and good breaks are in your DNA. Now, get rid of a chicken mentality and start having an eagle mentality.

Remind Yourself of Who You Are

I know a young lady who was raised in a single-parent home in public housing. Her mother wasn't around much when she was growing up. They were very poor. At sixteen years old, this young lady got pregnant and had to drop out of school. At one time she'd had a big dream for her life. She knew she was going to be something great, but now it looked as though the cycle of lack and defeat would be passed to the next generation. She moved into a tiny apartment to try to raise her son, but she couldn't make ends meet. She had to go on welfare and found a job at a school cafeteria punching the meal tickets. She was earning minimum wage, barely making it through, but something deep down inside her said, "You were made for more. You're not a chicken. You're an eagle."

She decided to go back to school. In two years, she got her GED. That was good, but she wasn't satisfied. She enrolled in college, working during the day and going to class at night. In four years, she graduated from college with honors. She still wasn't satisfied. She went back and got her master's degree. Today, she is the assistant principal at the same school where she used to punch meal tickets. She said, "I used to be on welfare, but now I'm doing fair and well." That's what happens when you know who you are.

Now, you may work with a bunch of chickens. You may live in a neighborhood with chickens. You may have relatives who still think they're chickens. You must do what she did. Draw that line in the sand and say, "I may be in a limited environment, but I am not settling here. I know who I am. I am an eagle. I am a king's son. I am a mighty hero. I am a thoroughbred. I have winning in my DNA."

> *Draw that line in the sand and say, "I may be in a limited environment, but I am not settling here."*

Friend, you come from a bloodline of champions. Get up every morning and check your spiritual birth certificate. Remind yourself of who you are. If you do this, I believe and declare, you're going to soar to new heights. You're going to rise above every obstacle. You're going to set new levels for your family and become everything God has created you to be.

I AM
A MASTERPIECE

CHAPTER SEVEN

See Yourself as a Masterpiece

Too many people go around feeling wrong on the inside. They don't really like who they are. They think, *If I were just a little taller, if I had a better personality, if my metabolism were a little faster . . .* Or, *If I just looked like her, I would feel good about myself.*

But when God created you, He went to great lengths to make you exactly as He wanted. You didn't accidentally get your personality. You didn't just happen to get your height, your looks, your skin color, or your gifts. God designed you on purpose to be the way you are. You have what you need to fulfill your destiny. If you needed to be taller, God would have made you taller. If you needed to be a different nationality, God would have made you that way. If you needed to look like her instead of you, you would have looked like her. You have to be confident in who God made you to be.

Ephesians 2:10 says, "We are God's masterpiece." That means you are not ordinary. You didn't come off an assembly line. You weren't mass-produced. You are one of a kind. Nobody in this world has your fingerprints. There will never be another you. If you're going to reach your highest potential, you have to see yourself as unique, as an original, as God's very own masterpiece.

When I was in my early twenties, I was sitting by myself on the beach in India watching the sunset. It was a magnificent scene. The water was so blue. As far as I could see from the right to the left, there were miles and miles of beach and palm trees. The sun was huge on the horizon, just about to set. As I sat there reflecting, thinking about my life, I heard God ask me something—not out loud but just an impression down inside. He said, "Joel, you think this is a beautiful picture, do you?"

I replied, "Yes, God. I think this is a magnificent picture."

"Well," He asked, "what do you think would be My most prized painting, My most incredible creation?"

I thought about it a moment and answered, "God, it must be this sunset. This is breathtaking."

"No, it's not this."

Earlier that year I had been in the Rocky Mountains. They were spectacular. I continued, "God, I bet it's the Rocky Mountains."

"No, not that."

I wondered out loud, "What could it be? The solar system? The Milky Way?"

> *"My most prized possession, the painting that I'm the most proud of, is you."*

He responded, "No, Joel. My most prized possession, the painting that I'm the most proud of, is you."

I thought, *Me? It couldn't be me. I'm ordinary. I'm just like everybody else.*

He said, "You don't understand. When I made the solar system, the waters, and the mountains, I was proud of that. That was great. But Joel, when I made you, I breathed My very life into you. I created you in My own image."

You Are God's Most Prized Possession

Friend, you are God's most prized possession. Don't go around feeling wrong about yourself. Quit wishing you were taller, or had a better personality, or looked like somebody else. You've been painted by the most incredible painter there could ever be. When God created you, He stepped back and looked and said, "That was good. Another masterpiece!" He stamped His approval on you.

On the inside of our shirts there's usually a tag that reads, "Made in America" or some other country. Well, somewhere on you, there's a tag that states, "Made by Almighty God." So put your shoulders back and hold your head up high. You are extremely valuable. When those thoughts come telling you everything that you're not, remind yourself, "I have the fingerprints of God all over me—the way I look, the way I smile, my gifts, my personality. I know I am not average. I am a masterpiece." Those are the thoughts that should be playing in your mind all day long. Not *I am slow. I am unattractive. I am just one of the seven billion people on Earth.* No, God did not make anything average. If you have breath to breathe, you are a masterpiece.

Now, people may try to make you feel average. Your own thoughts may try to convince you that you are ordinary. Life will try to push you down and steal your sense of value. That's why all through the day you have to remind yourself of who your Painter is. When you dwell on the fact that Almighty God breathed His life into you and approved you, equipped you, and empowered you, then any thoughts of low self-esteem and inferiority don't have a chance.

A few years ago I was in somebody's home. They had many paintings on the walls, which weren't very impressive to me. In fact, some of them looked as if they had been painted by a child—very abstract, modern, paint thrown here and there. But later that evening, they mentioned how they had paid more than a million dollars for just one of those paintings. I looked at it again and thought, *Wow! That is beautiful, isn't it?*

Come to find out, it was an original Pablo Picasso. What dawned on me that night was that it's not so much what the painting looks

> *It's not so much what the painting looks like. It's who the painter is.*

like. It's who the painter is. The painting gets its value from its creator. In the same way, our value doesn't come from how we look or what we do or who we know. Our value comes from the fact that Almighty God is our Painter. So don't criticize what God has painted. Accept yourself. Approve yourself. You are not an accident. You have been fearfully and wonderfully made.

I wonder what would happen if all through the day, instead of putting ourselves down, instead of dwelling on the negative, we would go around thinking, *I am a masterpiece. I am wonderfully made. I am talented. I am an original. I have everything that I need.* The enemy doesn't want you to feel good about yourself. He would love for you to go through life listening to the nagging voices that remind you of everything that you are not. I dare you to get up each day and say, "Good morning, you wonderful thing!" You are fearfully and wonderfully made.

How many of us are bold enough to say as David did in Psalm 139, "I am amazing. I am a masterpiece." Those thoughts never enter into most people's minds. They're too busy putting themselves down, focusing on their flaws, comparing themselves to others whom they think are better. Your Painter, your Creator, says, "You're amazing. You're wonderful. You're a masterpiece." Now it's up to you to get in agreement with God. If you go around focused on your flaws, listening to what other people are saying, you can miss your destiny. The recording that should be playing in our mind all day long is, "I am

valuable. I am a masterpiece. I am a child of the Most High God."
Could it be this is what's holding you back? Your recording is negative. There are enough people in life already against you. Don't be
against yourself. Change your recording. Start seeing yourself as the
masterpiece God created you to be.

Realize What You Have

I read a story about a man who died in extreme poverty. At one
point, he was homeless, living on the streets, and barely getting by
in life. After the funeral, some of his relatives went to his run-down
apartment and gathered up his belongings. He had a painting on the
wall, which they sold at a garage sale. The person who bought the
painting took it to the local art gallery to learn more about it. They
discovered it had been painted back in the 1800s by a famous artist and was extremely valuable. It ended up selling at an auction for
more than three million dollars. That man lived his whole life in
poverty because he didn't realize what he had.

In the same way, every one of us has been painted by the most
famous Artist there could ever be. But
if you don't understand your value, you
go around thinking, *I'm just average.*
I'm not that talented. I've made a lot of
mistakes in life. If you let that negative
recording play, you're just like the man

> *Every one of us has*
> *been painted by the most*
> *famous Artist there*
> *could ever be.*

with the painting—you have everything you need and you're full of
potential, but you'll never tap into it. That's why every morning you
need to remind yourself, "I am not average. I am not ordinary. I have
the fingerprints of God all over me. I am a masterpiece."

There was an article in a medical magazine that talked about how researchers had scientifically calculated how much money the human body is worth. They added up the cost of all the enzymes, cells, tissues, organs, hormones; everything contained in the body. They concluded that an average-sized person is worth six million dollars. You've heard of the "Six Million Dollar Man." Well, you are a Six Million Dollar Person. You can put your shoulders back. You can have a spring in your step. Your Heavenly Father has invested six million dollars in you. The good news is you didn't even have to pay taxes on it!

Think of this: Six million dollars is the worth of an average-sized person. You may be worth nine million dollars! That's the way to look at it. You're not overweight. You're just more valuable.

Be Proud of Who God Made You to Be

Jesus said to love your neighbor as you love yourself. If you don't love yourself in a healthy way, you will never be able to love others in the way that you should. This is why some people don't have good relationships. If you don't get along with yourself, you'll never get along with others. We all have weaknesses, shortcomings, things that we wish were different. But God never designed us to go through life being against our self. The opinion you have of yourself is the most important opinion that you have. If you see yourself as less than, not talented, not valuable, you will become exactly that. You are constantly conveying what you feel on the inside. Even subconsciously, you're sending messages out. If you feel unattractive on the inside, you can be the most beautiful person in the world, but you will convey feelings of unattractiveness. That's going to push people away. The problem is inside. You carry yourself the way you see yourself.

I've seen just the opposite happen. A few years ago I met a young lady who, on the surface, and I say this respectfully, wasn't necessarily attractive. She didn't have a lot of what today's culture defines as natural beauty, but I can tell you that inside she had it going on! She knew she was made in the image of Almighty God. She knew she was crowned with favor. She may have looked ordinary, but she thought extraordinary. She carried herself like a queen and walked like she was royalty. She smiled like she was Miss America and dressed like she was headed for the runway. She may have bought her outfit at a secondhand store, but she wore it as though it were brand-new from Saks Fifth Avenue. All I could say was, "You go, girl!"

What was the difference? On the inside she saw herself as beautiful, strong, talented, and valuable. What's on the inside will eventually show up on the outside. Because she saw herself as a masterpiece, she exuded strength, beauty, and confidence.

Here's a key: People see you the way you see yourself. If you see yourself as strong, talented, and valuable, that's the way other people will see you. That's the messages you're sending out. But if you see yourself as

> People see you the way you see yourself.

less than, not talented, and not valuable, that's the way others will see you. Perhaps if you would change the opinion you have of yourself, if you would quit focusing on your flaws and everything you wish was different, if you would quit comparing yourself to somebody else who you think is better and start loving yourself in a healthy way, being proud of who God made you to be, then as you send out these different messages, it's going to bring new opportunities, new relationships, and new levels of God's favor.

This is what the Israelites did. When ten of the spies came back from the Promised Land, they saw how huge their opponents were.

They said to Moses, "We were in our own sights as grasshoppers, and so we were in their sights."

Notice they didn't say, "Moses, those people insulted us. They called us grasshoppers." They went in with a grasshopper mentality. They said, "We were in our own sights as grasshoppers." That's what they conveyed. Here's the principle at work: "And so we were in their sights." In other words, "They saw us the way we saw ourselves."

If you project feelings of inferiority, people will treat you as inferior. You may feel that you have a disadvantage similar to the Israelites. You don't have the size, the talent, or the education. That's all right. All that matters is Almighty God breathed His life into you. He created you as a person of destiny. He put seeds of greatness inside you. Now do your part. Start seeing yourself as the masterpiece God created you to be.

You Are Royalty

The Scripture talks about how God has made us to be kings and priests unto Him. Men, you need to start seeing yourself as a king. Women, start seeing yourself as a queen. Start carrying yourself as royalty. Not with arrogance, thinking that you're better than others, but in humility be proud of who God made you to be. You are not better than anyone else, but you are not less than anyone else either. It doesn't matter how many degrees they have. It doesn't matter how important their family is. Understand, your Father created the whole universe. When He breathed His life into you and sent you to planet Earth, you didn't come as ordinary. You didn't come as average. He put a

> *Start thinking as royalty, talking as royalty, walking as royalty, and acting as royalty.*

crown of honor on your head. Now, start thinking as royalty, talking as royalty, walking as royalty, and acting as royalty.

I was in England a few years ago. They were having a ceremony to honor the queen. When the queen walked in the room, you could feel the strength, the confidence, and the dignity. She had her head held high and a pleasant smile on her face. She waved to everyone as though they were her best friends. What was interesting was that there were all kinds of important people in that room. There were presidents of other nations, world-renowned entertainers, famous athletes, scientists, and some of the brightest, most talented people in the world. But—and I say this respectfully—the queen was not the most beautiful person in the room. There were other ladies who were younger and much more beautiful, but judging from the way the queen carried herself, you would have thought she was the cat's meow. She had it going on—strong, confident, secure. The queen wasn't the wealthiest, fittest, or most educated woman in the room either. A lot of people would have been intimidated walking into that room, but not her. She walked in as though she owned the place. Why? She knows who she is. She's the queen. She comes from a long line of royalty. It's been ingrained in her thinking, *I'm not average. I'm not ordinary. I am one of a kind.*

No doubt some mornings when the queen wakes up, the same thoughts come to her mind that come to all of us. *You're not as beautiful as your sister. You're not as talented as your brother. You're not as smart as your coworker. Be intimidated. You're inferior.* The queen lets that go in one ear and out the other. She thinks, *What are you talking about? It doesn't matter how I compare to others. I'm the queen. I've got royalty in my blood. In my DNA is generations of influence, honor, and prestige.*

If you and I could ever start seeing ourselves as the kings and the queens God made us to be, we would never be intimidated again.

You don't have to be the most talented to feel good about yourself. You don't have to be the most educated or the most successful. When you understand your Heavenly Father breathed His life into you, you too come from a long line of royalty. Instead of being intimidated or made to feel insecure by someone who you think is more important, you can do like the queen. Just be at ease, be kind, be confident, and be friendly, knowing that you are one of a kind. Ladies, you may not be the most beautiful person, but be confident you're the queen. Men, you may not be the most successful, but stand up tall. You're the king. You are crowned not by people but by Almighty God.

But a lot of times we think, *I can't feel good about myself. I've got this addiction. I struggle with a bad temper. I've made a lot of mistakes in life. I don't feel like a masterpiece.* Here's the key: Your value is not based on your performance. You don't have to do enough good and then maybe God will approve you. God has already approved you.

Dare to Believe You Are Excellent

When Jesus was being baptized by John in the Jordan River, He hadn't started His ministry yet. He had never opened one blind eye, never raised the dead, never turned water into wine. He had not performed a single miracle. But a voice boomed out of the heavens, and God said, "This is My beloved Son in whom I am well pleased." His Father was pleased with Him because of who He was and not because of anything He had or had not done.

We tell ourselves, "If I could break this addiction, I'd feel good about myself. If I could read my Bible more, if I could bite my tongue and not argue so much, maybe I wouldn't be against myself." You have to learn to accept yourself while you're in the process of changing. We all have areas we need to improve, but we're not supposed to go around down on ourselves because we haven't arrived. When you're against yourself, it doesn't help you to do better. It makes you do worse. You may have a bad habit you know you need to overcome, but if you go around feeling guilty and condemned, thinking about all the times you've failed, the times you've blown it, that will not motivate you to go forward. You have to shake off the guilt. Shake off the condemnation. You may not be where you want to be, but you can look back and thank God you're not where you used to be. You're growing. You're making progress. Do yourself a big favor and quit listening to the accusing voices. That's the enemy trying to convince you to be against yourself. He knows that if you don't like yourself, you will never become who God created you to be.

In Genesis 1, God had just created the heavens, the earth, the sea, the animals, and Adam and Eve. When He finished, the Scripture says, "God

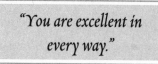

"You are excellent in every way."

looked over all that He had made and saw how it was excellent in every way." When God looks at you, He says, "You are excellent in every way."

You may think, *Not me, I've got these bad habits, these shortcomings. I've made some mistakes in the past.* Get out of that defeated mentality. You may not be perfect, but God is not basing your value on your performance. He's looking at your heart. He is looking at the fact that you're trying. You wouldn't be reading this if you didn't have a heart to please God. Now, quit being down on yourself. Quit living condemned, and dare to believe you are excellent in every way. Our attitude should be, *Yes, I may make some mistakes. I have some flaws and weaknesses, but I am not going to live my life guilty, condemned. I know God has already approved me. I am excellent in every way. I am His masterpiece.*

If you're going to overcome your flaws and weaknesses, you have to not only stay positive toward yourself, but be bold enough to celebrate who God made you to be. Be proud of who you are. I know people who are good at celebrating others. They'll compliment their friends and brag on a cousin. "You have to see my neighbor. He's an awesome football player. You must meet my sister. She is so beautiful." And that's good. We should celebrate others, but make sure you also celebrate yourself. You are smart. You are talented. You are beautiful. There is something special about you. You can't get so caught up in celebrating others, putting them on a pedestal, to where you think, *They are so great, and I am so average. She is so beautiful, and I am so plain.*

They may have more natural beauty or more talent in some area, but God didn't leave anybody out. You have something that they don't have. You're good at something that they're not good at. And it's fine to celebrate them and say, "Wow! Look how great they are," as long as you follow it up by saying internally, "And you know what? I'm great, too. I'm smart, too. I'm talented, too."

One of a Kind

It's like this story I heard about the mayor of a small town. He was in a parade, riding in a float down Main Street with his wife next to him. While he was waving to all the different people, he spotted in the crowd his wife's former boyfriend, who owned and ran the local gas station. The mayor whispered to his wife, "Aren't you glad you didn't marry him? You'd be working at a gas station."

> *"No. If I would've married him, he'd be the mayor."*

She whispered back, "No. If I would've married him, he'd be the mayor."

You have to know who you are. God breathed His life into you. You have royalty in your blood. You are excellent in every way. Now, put your shoulders back, hold your head up high, and start carrying yourself as royalty. You are not average. You are not ordinary. You are a masterpiece. Get up every morning and remind yourself of who your Painter is. Your value doesn't come because of who you are. It comes because of whose you are. Remember, the most important opinion is the opinion you have of yourself. How you see yourself is how other people are going to see you. I'm asking you today to see yourself as a king. See yourself as a queen. Not arrogantly but in humility, for that is truly who you are.

Maybe you need to change the recording that's playing in your mind. If the message is, *I'm slow. I'm unattractive. I'm nothing special*, dare to say, like David, "I am amazing. I am talented. I am one of a kind. I am a masterpiece."

CHAPTER EIGHT

Living Content

I t's good to have dreams and goals. We should be stretching our faith, believing for something bigger. But here's the key: While we're waiting for things to change, waiting for promises to come to pass, we shouldn't be discontent where we are. Maybe you're believing to have a baby, believing for a new house, or believing to get married. That's great, but don't go the next five years discontent being single, discontent with the house you have, or discontent not having a child. Learn to enjoy the season that you're in.

Being unhappy, frustrated, and wondering if something is ever going to change is not going to make it happen any sooner. When we're discontent, we're dishonoring God. We're so focused on what we want that we're taking for granted what we have. The right attitude is, *God, I'm believing for a new house, but in the meantime I'm happy with the house I have. I'm believing to get married, but in the meantime I'm content being single. I'm believing for a better job, but I'm happy with the job I have right now.*

The Apostle Paul said, "I have *learned* how to be content, whether I'm abased or abounding, whether I have plenty

> "I have learned *how to be content.*"

or whether I'm in need." Notice he had to *learn* to be content. It doesn't happen automatically. It's a choice we have to make.

Being content doesn't mean that we don't want change, that we give up on our dreams, or that we settle where we are. It means we're not fighting everything. We're not frustrated. We're trusting God's timing. We know He is working behind the scenes, and at the right time He will get us to where we're supposed to be.

I've found some situations will not change until we change. As long as we're frustrated, stressed out, thinking, *Why is it taking so long? Why am I still dealing with this problem? Why is my husband still aggravating me?* nothing will change.

But if God has us in a situation, we must need to be there. He is going to use it to do a work in us. When we're content, we're growing. We're developing character. Our faith is being strengthened. You don't grow as much in the good times, when everything is going your way. You grow when there's pressure. You feel like being sour, but you choose to be happy. You could easily complain, but you say, "Lord, thank You for another great day." All of your dreams haven't come to pass, but you choose to enjoy the season that you're in. That's passing the test. That's what allows God to go to work. Instead of trying to change the situation, let it change you. There's something wrong if we're always discontented. "I don't like my job. I'm tired of this small apartment. I don't have enough help with the kids. When is my business ever going to grow?" That's going to keep you where you are. God's plan for our life is not to just make us comfortable but to grow us up, to mature us, so He can release more of His favor. You may not like where you are, but you wouldn't be there unless God had a purpose for it. Make sure you pass the test.

Bloom Where You're Planted

This is what David did. He spent years in the lonely shepherd's fields taking care of his father's sheep. What's interesting is that he had already been chosen to be the next king of Israel. The prophet Samuel had already anointed him. David could have thought, *God, this isn't right. I've got big dreams. You promised me great things. What am I doing stuck out here with a bunch of sheep?*

But David understood this principle. He didn't live stressed or frustrated. He bloomed where he was planted. He knew that God was in control, so he just kept being his best, going to work with a good attitude, grateful for where he was. Because he was content in the shepherd's fields, he made it to the throne, to the palace. He passed that test. But if you're not content in the season you're in, while you're waiting for things to change, then even if you do somehow make it to your throne, so to speak, and your dreams do come to pass, you're still not going to be satisfied. You may be happy for a little while, but here's the problem: Discontentment will follow you everywhere you go.

> *Discontentment will follow you everywhere you go.*

A few years ago I came home one evening, and I heard this high-pitched sound in the house, like a tone you hear from a television broadcast. I could just faintly hear it. I thought maybe a smoke detector battery was low or an alarm was going off upstairs. So I started going around everywhere, trying to figure out where it was. But it seemed as though everywhere I went, it sounded exactly the same. I couldn't get any closer to it. It was very puzzling. I went upstairs and checked rooms and drawers, checked the pantry. Finally, I went up in the attic. I thought maybe a hot water heater or an air conditioner had a part that was going bad. I got way up in the attic, and it still sounded exactly the same. After about twenty minutes, I went down to my room to change clothes. I took off my cell phone from my belt where it was clipped, and I put it on my counter. When I did, I could tell the tone was coming from my cell phone! That's why it sounded the same everywhere I went. It was clipped to me. I couldn't get away from it.

That's the way it is with discontentment. It follows us around. If God blesses us with a promotion, we're happy for a little while, but then the discontentment comes. We don't want to work so hard or we don't want the responsibility. But it's not our circumstances. It's the spirit of discontentment, seeing the wrong, complaining about what we don't like, never having enough. That's why Paul said, "I've *learned* how to be content." You have to train your mind to see the good, to be grateful for what you have. Life will go so much better if you will be content in each season. Content when you have a lot, and content when you don't have a lot. Content whether your children are in diapers or whether they're in college. Content whether you're in maintenance or management.

You have the grace you need to enjoy each season. If your dreams are not coming to pass, that's a test. Will you do as David did and bloom where you're planted? Will you choose to enjoy that season and not just endure it, thinking, *God, when is this ever going to change? I've been praying for two years.* Maybe your situation is going to change when you change. You have to be satisfied with where God has you right now. Again, it doesn't mean you settle there and never expect anything better. It means you don't live frustrated, always wanting something more. "I need more money. Then I'll be happy." "I need a better job." "I need a bigger house." "I need

> *Maybe your situation is going to change when you change.*

to lose twenty pounds." "I need my kids to make better grades. Then I'll enjoy life."

If you get all that corrected, if you accomplish your wish list, something else will come up to make you discontented. You have to put your foot down and say, "That's it. Everything may not be perfect in my life. All my dreams may not have come to pass yet, but I'm not living frustrated and stressed out. I'm going to bloom right where I'm planted." In other words, "I'm content whether I'm driving a twenty-year-old Volkswagen or a brand-new Mercedes Benz." "I'm content whether I'm living in a small apartment or a beautiful dream house." "I'm content whether my business is booming or whether it's a little slow."

It's Not About What You Have or Don't Have

You cannot let your contentment be based on what you have or don't have, on who likes you or who doesn't like you. Learn to be content in every season. Content when God blesses you with a lot, and content when you have a little. Content when the dreams are coming to pass, and content while you're waiting. Content in the shepherd's fields, and content in the palace. The Scripture says, "Godliness with contentment is great gain." Life is very freeing when you can say, "I'm content with who God made me to be. I'm content with my personality, content with my looks, and content with my gifts. I'm content with where I am in life—my position, my career, my relationships, and my house."

This is the reason many people are unhappy. They're always wishing for something different. Some single people are not going to be content until they get married. But you need to enjoy being single because when you get married... you'll enjoy it more! (I'm smarter than I look.) There are married people who wish they weren't married, or who wish they were married to somebody else. White people sit in tanning booths trying to get darker. Dark people put cream on their skin trying to get lighter. Ladies with curly hair go to the salon to get it straightened. People with straight hair go to the salon to get it permed. People with no hair go to the salon to buy some hair!

Of course, there's nothing wrong with improving, being your best, and showing your style, but you shouldn't always be wishing you were something different. Be content with who God made you to be. It's a tragedy to go through life always dissatisfied, wishing you had more, wanting to look like somebody else, waiting to be happy. I'm asking you to be content right where you are.

Think about Mary, the mother of Christ. When she was pregnant with Jesus, she had to ride a donkey to Bethlehem. Now, I've lived with a pregnant woman twice. If I would have suggested that Victoria get on a donkey at nine months pregnant, I probably wouldn't be writing this. Mary could have complained, "Joseph, why don't you get me something smoother? This is hard." When she got to Bethlehem, "Joseph, why didn't you make us a hotel reservation? Why didn't you get me a hospital room? You knew I was going to have this baby. It's been all over the news." When the baby was born, "Joseph, why didn't you buy the baby a new outfit? I have to wrap my beautiful baby in swaddling clothes." That means strips of cloth. Mary didn't have designer jeans, a fancy purse, or a latte from Starbucks. But she never complained. She never found fault with Joseph.

Mary didn't say, "God, if I'm going to have this baby for You, at least You could make it more comfortable on me." She was content in the season she was in, content when the angel said, "You've been highly favored," and content riding a donkey while pregnant, content giving birth in a barn with a bunch of animals, and content when the wise men said, "Your son is the Messiah." It takes a mature person to be content on the mountaintop and content in the valley.

> *It takes a mature person to be content on the mountaintop and content in the valley.*

Learn to Be Content

A couple of years after Victoria and I were married, we found a piece of property that we really liked. It was close into the city and in a nice neighborhood, but it had a very old run-down house on it that had major foundation problems. Most people would have torn it down, but we decided to fix it up and live in it. The floors in the den were so slanted that I had to put little blocks of wood under the front legs of the couch so it would be level with the back legs. Most of the interior doors would not close properly. That didn't bother us. We were happy.

My mother would come over to our house and say, "Joel, how do you live in this house with these crooked floors?" But I've learned that God gives you the grace for each season. Today, we have a nice house with level floors. But I don't believe we would be where we are if we had not been content in that older home. It would have been easy to complain, "This is a piece of junk. God, we wanted something new. When is it ever going to change?" No; pass the test. Whether you're abased or abounding, whether you're in your dream house or a crooked-floor house, make the decision: "I'm going to be content. I'm going to enjoy my life. I'm going to be grateful for what God has given me. I'm going to be the best I can be right where I am."

Paul, who said, "I've *learned* how to be content," wrote much of the New Testament from a prison cell. When you've made up your mind to be content, prisons can't stop you, crooked floors can't stop you, donkeys can't stop you, lonely shepherds' fields can't stop you. God will get you to where you're supposed to be.

A gentleman recently was telling me about all of his problems and about everything that was wrong in his life and went on and on. It was a long story. He ended by saying, "Joel, I just don't like my life." Here's the problem. It's the only life you have. You can't trade it in. You can't become someone else. You may have a thousand reasons to live unhappily, but you have to make the choice that you're going to be content. If you're sour and complain, "When is it ever going to change?" you'll get stuck. God does not promote discontentment. Shake it off and focus on what's right in your life. Focus on what you do have. When we woke up this morning, most of us could see the sunlight—our eyes worked. Most of us could hear the birds sing-

Don't miss the gift of this day.

ing. We had a roof over our heads. We have opportunities and people to love in our lives. There's a lot right in your life. Don't take it for granted. Don't get so focused on the crooked floors, the donkeys, and the struggles that you miss the gift of this day.

Enjoy the Season You're In

Every season is not springtime, with the beautiful blooming flowers, gorgeous sunshine, and cool weather. That's a great season, but you're not going to grow if you stay in harvest. There has to be planting seasons, watering seasons, and maintaining seasons, when you're pulling the weeds and tilling the soil. Those are important seasons. Without going through that process, you're not going to come into a new season of harvest. Instead of being frustrated by the difficulties, have a new perspective. The season you're in is getting you prepared for promotion. It may look as though you're stuck. You don't see anything happening, but God is at work, and at the right time the season will change. Winter always gives way to spring. It takes a mature person to be content not only in the harvest season but content in the planting season, content in the watering season, and content in the "pulling up the weeds" season.

You may be in one of those difficult seasons right now, raising a small child, taking care of an elderly loved one, or perhaps dealing with an illness. You feel like you're riding that donkey. It's easy to think, *As soon as I get through this tough time, I'll get my joy back. As soon as my kids get out of diapers...As soon as I make it through the busy season at work...As soon as I lose twenty pounds...* No, this is the day the Lord has made. You have to choose to rejoice today.

God has given you the grace you need to not only endure this season—that doesn't take any faith—but to also enjoy the season. When you're content, you see each day as a gift. You appreciate the people in your life. You're grateful for what God has given you. You're not only getting stronger and developing your character, but you're also passing the test. You will come out of fall and winter, and come into your springtime. Things will begin to bloom and blossom once again.

When I was growing up, there were five of us kids in the house. My parents were pastors. We didn't have a lot of money, but as a little boy I always felt as though we were well off. We had fun. We played hide-and-seek in the house. We would go out in the front yard and have races. Life was good. My parents couldn't afford to take us on a big family vacation every year, so every couple of months my father would load us kids up in the car and take us out to the airport to ride the tram from Terminal A to Terminal B! There were just two terminals back then, and the tram was *free*. We thought that was so great. We would ride it over and over and over. People would look at us like we were confused. But we weren't lost; we were having fun. My father learned to be content in each season. Instead of complaining that he didn't have enough, he chose to bloom right where he was planted.

It's funny. When some of my childhood friends would tell me they were going to Disneyland, I always thought that meant they were going to the airport to ride the trams. I'd say, "Yeah, we've been there before." When I got old enough to realize what Disneyland really was, I needed counseling!

Life Is Never Problem Free

Don't miss a great season in your life wishing you had more, complaining about what you don't have. The real joy in life is in the simple things—making memories with

> The real joy in life is in the simple things.

your family, riding the trams together at the airport, playing hide-and-seek in the house, watching the sunset with your spouse, and staring up at the stars at night.

When our son, Jonathan, was five and Alexandra was two, we planned a big vacation to Disneyland. They were going to get to eat breakfast with Mickey Mouse and take pictures with the other characters. It was a big deal, getting the flights with two small children out to California, booking the hotel, and picking up the rental car. I spent half of my retirement to get there!

After we checked into the hotel, we went straight to the park. I was so excited for my children. But we weren't there fifteen minutes when Jonathan said, "Dad, I want to go back to the hotel and go swimming."

I didn't think I heard him right. I asked, "You want to do what?"

"I want to go back and go swimming."

"No, no, no, Jonathan," I replied. "We're at Disneyland. We came a long way. Look at all these rides. Isn't this going to be fun?"

"No," he spoke firmly. "Daddy, I want to go back and go swimming."

"Jonathan," I started to plead, "we can swim anytime at home at the neighborhood pool. We're at Disneyland!"

Jonathan sat down on the pavement, crossed his arms, and in no uncertain terms declared, "I don't want to be at Disneyland. I want to go swimming!"

"Jonathan," I exclaimed, "I spent fifty bucks on your ticket! You're going to have fun whether you like it or not!" I thought later, *I should have done what my dad did and taken them to the airport to ride the trams.* It could have saved me a lot of money!

You don't have to have a big vacation to have fun. Learn to enjoy the simple things in life. A mistake we make too often is that we think that when we reach a certain goal, then we'll be happy. "As soon as I finish college..." "As soon as I get the promotion..." "As soon as I move into the new house..." "As soon as I have this baby, I'll enjoy my life." Yes, you'll be happy when you accomplish your goals, but there are challenges that come along with it. I've heard it said, "With every blessing comes a burden." You'll never come to a place where you're problem free, having no conflicts and no bills to pay, and everybody is celebrating you. That's not reality. If you don't learn to be content where you are, you won't be content when your dreams come to pass. When God blesses you with that new house, what comes with it is a bigger yard to mow, more rooms to clean, more to maintain. When you're blessed with that promotion, what comes with it is more responsibility. When you have that beautiful baby, there's nothing like it in all the world, but at three o'clock in the morning that baby wants to eat. They don't do things on our timetable. Don't pray for a bigger blessing if you're going to complain about a bigger burden.

We love our new church facility. It's a dream come true. God did more than we could ask or think. But with this amazing blessing came an amazing utility bill. The first time I saw it, I thought, *God, I sure liked our old facility.* The good news is that God wouldn't give you the blessing if you couldn't handle the burden. You have the grace you need for each season. Now, do your part and choose to be content. You could be in one of the best seasons of your life right now, but you're not enjoying it because you're focused on the burden, on

> *You have the grace you need for each season.*

what you don't have, on how difficult it is. Because you're waiting for things to change, you're missing the beauty of this moment, the joy of today. Don't go through life always wanting something else. See the gift in what you have right now. Can I tell you, we are living in the good old days. Twenty years from now you'll look back and say, "Wow! That was one of the best times of my life." Don't miss it living discontentedly.

See the Good

Mitch Albom is a great writer. He wrote a book called *The Five People You Meet in Heaven.* You may have seen the movie. Although it's not what the Scripture teaches about the afterlife, it makes a great point. It's about a man in his sixties who had worked at an amusement park his whole life. His parents owned it, and that's all he knew. He never really wanted to be there. He had dreams to do something bigger with his life, but unfortunate things kept happening. He found himself back at the amusement park—discontented, unfulfilled, never feeling it was where he was supposed to be, dreading going to work each day. On the outside he was kind and generous to people. He would go out of his way to help others, but inside he was unhappy and felt like a failure in life.

At one point there was a little girl on a ride who was in danger, about to be harmed. He rushed over to help her and saved the little girl's life, but in the process he was killed. He went to Heaven and was told that he would meet five people. These people would be instrumental in helping him to choose what kind of Heaven he would have. If he wanted to live on a beach, in a palace, or in the mountains, it was his choice.

One person he met was a man he had helped during the war. The man told him how much he meant to him. He then met three other people to whom he had been good. They expressed their heartfelt love and appreciation for what he had done. The last one he met was the little girl whose life he had saved. He began to realize that during all of his time on Earth he had felt as though he was at the wrong place and in the wrong job, but actually he was at the right place. God had been directing his steps. He had made a difference with his life. When he stepped back and saw it from a new perspective, he chose his Heaven to be the amusement park, the place that he had dreaded all those years.

Could it be that you're at the right place for the season that you're in, but you're not enjoying it? Maybe like him, if you would step back and see it from a new perspective, you would realize that God has you in the palm of His hand. He is directing your steps. He knows where you are, what you like, and what you don't like. Instead of living discontentedly, frustrated, always wishing you were somewhere else, embrace the place where you are. See the good. Be grateful for what you have. Remember, there is a blessing and a burden for every season. Don't focus on the burden. You have the grace to enjoy the blessing.

I AM
SECURE

CHAPTER NINE

Be Comfortable with Who You Are

There is an underlying pressure in our society to be number one. If we're not the best, the leader, the fastest, the most talented, the most beautiful, or the most successful, we're taught to not feel good about ourselves. We have to work harder. We have to run faster. We must stay ahead.

If a neighbor moves into a new house, instead of being inspired and happy for them, we're intimidated into thinking, *That's making me look bad. I've got to keep up.* If a coworker gets a promotion, we feel as though we're falling behind. We know we don't measure up when a friend tells us they're going to Europe on vacation, and we're going to our grandmother's twelve miles down the road.

If we're not careful, there will always be someone or something making us feel we're not up to par. We're not far enough along. As long as you compare your situation to others, you will never feel good about yourself, because there will always be somebody more talented, more beautiful, more successful.

> *As long as you compare your situation to others, you will never feel good about yourself.*

You have to realize you're not running their race. You're running your race. You have a specific assignment. God has given you exactly what you need for the race that's been designed for you. A friend, a coworker, or a relative may seem to have a more significant gift. They can outrun you and outperform you. That's okay. You're not competing with them. They have what they need for their assignment. You have what you need for your assignment.

Don't make the mistake of trying to keep up with them, wondering, *Why can't I sing like that? Why can't I be the manager? When am I going to reach their level?* If you're not content with your gift, comfortable with who God made you to be, you'll go through life frustrated and envious, thinking, *I wish I had her looks. I wish I had his talent. I wish I owned their business.* No, if you had what they have, it wouldn't help you; it would hinder you. They have a different assignment.

Quit trying to outperform others, and then you'll start to feel good about yourself. Don't condition your contentment upon moving into a new neighborhood, having your business catch up to someone else's, or getting a promotion. One of the best things I've ever learned is to be comfortable with who God made me to be. I don't have to outperform anyone to feel good about myself. I don't have to outbuild, outdrive, outrace, out-minister, or outproduce anyone. It's not about anyone else. It's about becoming who God made me to be.

> *I don't have to outbuild, outdrive, outrace, out-minister, or outproduce anyone.*

Accept the Gift God Has Given You

I'm all for having goals, stretching, and believing big. That's important. But you have to accept the gift that God has given you. You shouldn't feel less than if someone seems to have a more significant gift. It takes a secure person to say, "I'm comfortable with who I am."

I hear ministers who have deep voices and are great orators. They can move the congregation with their words and give you chill bumps, and I stand up in front of my congregation with my Texas twang. This is what I've been given. I can improve it. I can develop it. I can cultivate it, but my voice is never going to sound like James Earl Jones. There is always going to be somebody who can minister better, who is further along and more experienced. But you know what? That doesn't bother me. I know I have the gifts I need for my assignment.

Here's the key: You don't have to have a great gift for God to use it in a great way. Do you know what David's gift was that put him on the throne? It wasn't his leadership skills. It wasn't his dynamic personality. It wasn't his ability to write and play music. It was his gift to sling a rock. He was a sharpshooter with a slingshot. He could have thought, *Oh, great. Big deal. I'm good with a slingshot. This is not going to get me anywhere. I'm out in the shepherd's fields, alone, no people. Just a bunch of sheep.* But it was his slingshot, that seemingly insignificant gift, that enabled him to defeat Goliath and eventually put David on the throne.

Quit discounting the gift that God has given you. It may seem insignificant. "I'm not as smart as my sister. Not as talented as my coworker. Can't write the software like my colleague." Maybe not, but there's something God has given you that's unique, something that will propel you into your destiny, something that will cause you to leave your mark on this generation. Don't believe the lies that say, "You're average. There's nothing special about you. You don't have the personality that your cousin has. You don't have the talent of your friend." No, but you have a slingshot. It's not so much what you have; it's the anointing that God puts on it. That slingshot, your gift, may seem ordinary, but when God breathes on it, you'll defeat a giant twice your size. You'll be promoted beyond your talent. You'll go places where you weren't qualified. You didn't have the experience. You weren't next in line, but suddenly a door opened. Suddenly you defeated the giant. Suddenly the Compaq Center was yours. Suddenly the dream comes to pass.

Don't Wait for a Title or Position

Too often we pursue titles and positions, thinking we'll feel good about ourselves when we have them. "When I make it to sales manager, when I get on the varsity cheerleading squad, when I'm the head usher, the senior partner, the lead supervisor..." That's fine. There's nothing wrong with titles, but you don't need a title to do

> *Don't wait for people to approve you, affirm you, or validate you.*

what God has called you to do. Don't wait for people to approve you, affirm you, or validate you. Use your gift, and the title will come.

If David would have waited for a title, we wouldn't be talking about him today. When he went out to face Goliath, the whole army was watching him. And what's interesting is that David wasn't a general. He wasn't a corporal. He wasn't a sergeant. He wasn't even enlisted. He didn't have a title, a name badge, a uniform, or a single credential. He could have said, "I can't do anything great. I don't have a position. I am just a shepherd. Nobody is celebrating me. Nobody is validating my gifts." In fact, it was just the opposite. People were telling him how he was not qualified, how he was too small, how he was going to get hurt. That didn't bother David. His attitude was, *I don't need a title. I don't need a position. You didn't call me, and you don't have to approve me. God called me. He gave me this gift. It may seem small or insignificant to you, but I'm not here to impress you. I'm not here to please you. I'm here to fulfill my destiny.* He went out and defeated Goliath. In a few years they gave him a title: King of Israel. Use your gifts, and the titles will come.

"Well, Joel. As soon as they crown me King of the Office, I'll start being my best." "As soon as they make me the head usher, I'll show up early and give it my all." It works the other way around. You have to show them what you have, then the approval, then the recognition, then the reward will come.

When my father was seventeen years old, he gave his life to Christ, the first one in his family to do so. He knew that he was called to preach, but his family was very poor. They lost everything during the Great Depression, barely had enough food, and didn't have any money. He couldn't afford to go to college. He didn't have a position or title. No denomination was backing him up, and none of the family was saying, "John, follow your dreams. Do what's in your heart." His family told him, "John, you better stay here on the farm with us and pick cotton. You're going to get out there and fail."

Daddy could have thought, *I feel this calling. I know I have something to offer if somebody was just behind me.* But he didn't wait for a title or a position. He didn't wait for people to validate him. At seventeen, he started hitchhiking to different towns to minister in the seniors' homes, in the prisons, and on street corners. He used what he had. It didn't seem like much. Compared to other ministers who had been to seminary and had training, he would have been considered insignificant, unqualified, and inexperienced. But you can't wait for people's approval to do what God has called you to do.

What you have may seem small. You could feel intimidated, thinking that you don't have the qualifications, the title, the position.

That's okay. Neither did David. Neither did my father. If you'll use what you have, God will breathe on it. His anointing on that simple gift will cause you to step into the fullness of your destiny.

We Each Have Our Own Assignment

In the Scripture there was a little boy. All he had was a sack lunch—five loaves of bread, two fish. Nothing much. Not very significant. Yet, when thousands of people were hungry, Jesus took his lunch, multiplied it, and fed the whole crowd. Think about this. The little boy's mother got up early that morning to make the lunch. She baked the bread and cooked the fish, then she went out and picked some fruit off the tree, dug some vegetables out of the ground. She could have been considered insignificant. She was a homemaker raising a child. Other people were out doing more exciting things, being celebrated, making a splash. If she hadn't been comfortable with who she was, accepting her assignment, and secure in her gifts, she would have been out competing, trying to outperform others, thinking, *I'm falling behind. They're making me look bad. I'm just making a lunch. I don't have an important title.*

But titles don't bring fulfillment. Keeping up with your neighbors doesn't bring happiness. Trying to impress all your friends will make your life miserable, but running your race, understanding your assignment, and being comfortable with who God made you to be is what brings true

> *Titles don't bring fulfillment. Keeping up with your neighbors doesn't bring happiness.*

fulfillment. We hear a lot about the little boy being willing to give the lunch, but it all started when his mother took time to make the lunch. She used her gift that seemed small. Just making a lunch.

But God took the lunch, multiplied it, fed thousands, and we're still talking about it many years later.

Don't discount the gift God has given you. It may seem small just making a lunch for your children, but you don't know how God is going to use the child for whom you're making the lunch. You may be raising a president, a world leader, a great scientist, an entrepreneur, a business leader, or a pastor. You may not touch the world directly, but your child may change the world. Your assignment may be to help your seed go further. Are you secure enough to play the role that God has given you? Are you comfortable enough to not have to be number one, to be in the front, to have the title, the position, to keep up with others? We put so much emphasis on rising to the top, in being the leader. And yes, I believe in excelling and having big gifts and big dreams, but I also know that everyone can't be the leader. Everyone can't run the company. Everyone can't be on the platform. Somebody must open the doors. Somebody has to play the music. Somebody has to show people where to sit and where to park. The beauty of our God is that He has given us each an assignment. Every one of us has a specific gift and purpose.

What Is Your Assignment?

Think about this: Who was more important? The little boy with the lunch or the mother who made the lunch? Without the mother, we wouldn't be talking about the miracle. Who is more important? As the senior pastor, am I more important than the ones who open the building? Without them, we couldn't get in. Or is it the ones who turned on the lights, the sound system, and the cameras? Or perhaps the ones who paid the bills during the week? Or maybe it's the ones who poured the foundation some forty years ago and built the beautiful facility? Or maybe it's the ones who have supported the ministry down through the years? Here's the point. The answer is that we're all equally important. Without one, the whole thing wouldn't function properly. Be secure enough to play your role.

We look at who's in front, getting the credit and recognition. They're the leader. A lot of times we look up to them and admire them. That's where we want to be, but if that's not where we're called to be, if it's not where we're gifted, if it's not a part of our assignment, then we're going to be frustrated because it's not happening. If we do get there, we'll be frustrated trying to keep ourselves there, because if you promote yourself and manipulate your way into a position, you will have to constantly work to try to stay in that position. But where God takes you, He will keep you. Where you force your way, you have to keep yourself.

It's much better to have the attitude, *I don't have to be ahead of my friend to feel good about myself. I don't have to be on the main stage. I'm happy being in the background. I don't have to be the little boy with the lunch. I'm happy to be the mom who made the lunch. I'm happy to sing in the choir. I'm happy to make my company look good.*

When you're not competing, not comparing, not trying to be something that you're not, life gets a lot freer. It takes all the pressure off.

> When you're not competing, not comparing, not trying to be something that you're not, life gets a lot freer.

And yes, I realize there are some positions that carry more weight and more importance, but in God's eyes the usher is just as important as the pastor. The people who clean the building are just as important as the people who own the building. The secretary is just as important as the supervisor.

God is not going to judge you based on your neighbor's gift or your brother's gift or by how high you rose in the company. He is going to judge you based on the assignment that He has given you. Did you run your race? Not did you outperform your neighbor, were you more successful than your cousin, did you get more credit or recognition than your colleague? You're not competing with them. They're running a different race.

God is going to say to Queen Esther, "Did you have the courage to step up and save the nation as I gifted you to?" He is going to ask the little boy's mother, "Did you get up early and make the lunch as I gifted you to?" Two different assignments. Two different giftings. God is not going to compare. He's not going to say, "Oh, Esther. I'm prouder of you. You did so much more than the boy's mother who just made a little lunch." No, it's all going to be about whether or not we fulfilled our assignment.

Don't Be Distracted by Others

A few years ago I was out running. There was a man in front of me about a quarter of a mile who was running a little slower than me, so I decided to try to catch him. I had about a mile to go before I needed to turn off and head down my path. I picked up the pace, and I could tell every block that I was gaining on him. Within a few minutes I was only about a hundred yards behind him, and I started really pushing it. You would have thought I was in the final lap of the Olympic Games. I finally caught up to him, passed by him, and felt so good that I beat him. Of course, he didn't know we were racing! The funny thing is that when I got my mind back on what I was doing, I realized I had missed my turn. I was so focused on trying to catch him that I went about six blocks out of my way. I had to turn around and go back.

That's what happens when we're competing with other people,

trying to outperform them, dress better than them, make sure we're more successful. We end up competing in a race that we were never supposed to be in. Take the pressure off. It's very freeing to say, "I'm okay with you being ahead of me, getting more recognition, and doing something more exciting. I'm not going to feel bad about myself. If you have a bigger house, a badder car, and more success, you have what you need for your assignment. I have what I need for my assignment. I don't have to keep up with you. I'm not in the same race." You're not really free until you know you're not competing with anyone else.

> *You're not really free until you know you're not competing with anyone else.*

This is one of the reasons why King Saul lost the throne. He had been happy running his race. Life was good until he heard some women saying, "Saul has killed thousands, and David has killed tens of thousands." From that moment on, he never looked at David the same way. What was his problem? He couldn't handle somebody getting ahead of him. He was fine as long as he was number one, but he couldn't handle being number two. He got distracted and spent months and months trying to kill David, all because he wasn't comfortable with who he was.

Maybe like Saul you're at the one thousand level but you have a friend who's at the ten thousand level. The real test to see if God can promote you is, can you celebrate people who pass you by? Can you be happy for them and stay focused on your race, or does it frustrate you and cause you to think, *I've got to catch up with them.* Our attitude should be, *I may not be a ten-thousand-level person. God may have made me to be a one-thousand-level person, but I can promise you this: I'm going to be the best one-thousand-level person you've ever seen. I'm not going to stop at 950, 980, or 999. I'm going to become all God has created me to be.*

Don't Compare Yourself.
Celebrate Yourself.

Friend, your race is run by one person—you. Don't get distracted with competing against a neighbor, a friend, or a coworker. Just run your race. Here's a phrase I like: *Don't compare yourself. Celebrate yourself.*

Somebody else may have conquered ten thousand. You've conquered a thousand, but you know what? A thousand is still good. Celebrate what you've accomplished. Very few people today can say, "I like myself. I'm happy with my gifts. I am satisfied with who God made me to be." Remember, you don't have to have a great gift for God to use it in a great way. It may seem small, making a child's lunch or slinging a rock as David did, but when you use what you have, God will breathe on it and do amazing things.

I AM
VICTORIOUS

CHAPTER TEN

It's Under Your Feet

How we see our difficulties very often will determine whether we get out of them. When we face challenges and things come against us, it's easy to get overwhelmed and start thinking, *This is never going to work out. I'll just have to learn to live with it.* Many people settle for mediocrity. But Corinthians talks about how God has put all things under our feet. If you're going to live in victory, you have to see every sickness, every obstacle, and every temptation as being under your feet. Those things are no match for you. They're not going to keep you from your destiny. They've already been defeated. It's just a matter of time before you walk it out.

If you see a challenge as too big and say, "I'll never break this addiction. My child will never straighten up. This sickness is going to be the end of me," you're going to feel weak, discouraged, and intimidated. You're going to attract fear, worry, and doubt. That kind of thinking not only pushes you down, but it stops God from working. You have to change your perspective. That addiction is not going to dog you all of your life. It's under your feet. That depression that's been in your family for years, it's not going to get passed to the next generation. It's under your feet. You're going to put a stop to it.

The struggle, lack, and barely getting by are not going to keep you from being blessed. It's all under your feet. It's just a matter of time before you break through to a new level.

You have to shake off the lies that are telling you, "It's too big. It's

> *Shake off the lies that are telling you, "It's too big. It's been this way too long. It's never going to change."*

been this way too long. It's never going to change." This is a new day. God is saying, "Every enemy, every sickness, every obstacle; they're not going to defeat you. They're going to promote you." The difficulty was meant to be a stumbling block to keep you down, but God is going to use it as a stepping-stone to take you higher. Keep the right perspective. It's under your feet.

Make Sure You're Looking Down

This is what David did. He faced all kinds of enemies. He said in Psalm 59, "I will look down in triumph on *all* of my enemies." Notice that David did not say "some of my enemies." No; "all of my enemies." What am I going to do? Look down. Why? Because they're all under my feet.

You may be facing situations that don't feel like they're under your feet. The sickness looks big. The financial difficulty seems impossible. Perhaps you've struggled with an addiction for years. But you can't go by what you see. You must go by what you know. We walk by faith and not by sight. In the natural, it may look huge, but when you talk to those obstacles by faith, as David did, you need to look down. When you talk to God, you should look up. You look up to ask for help. But when you talk to sickness, look down. It's under your feet. Look down to talk to depression. Look down to talk to fear. I've heard it said, "If you want to say something to the enemy, write it on the bottom of your shoe, because he is under your feet."

On the day before a big boxing match, the two fighters will come out at a press conference and stand toe-to-toe with their faces just inches apart. They'll look each other in the eye and just stand there and stare and stare, trying to intimidate each other. They're saying, "I'm bigger, stronger, tougher, meaner. You're not going to

> *"If you want to say something to the enemy, write it on the bottom of your shoe, because he is under your feet."*

defeat me!" When you face an enemy, something that's trying to keep you from your destiny—a sickness, a bad habit, an unfair situation—unlike those two fighters, you don't stand toe-to-toe to look that enemy in the eye. That enemy is not at your level. It may have a big bark. It may seem so tough and so big that you can't defeat it. But the truth is, it's no match for you. For you to look that enemy in the eye, you need to look down under your feet. You are more than a conqueror. Greater is He that's in you than he that comes against you. The enemy has limited power. God has all power.

If God be for you, who dare be against you? Quit telling yourself, "I'll always struggle in this area. I'll never lose this weight. I'll never get out of debt." Change your perspective. You are not weak, defeated, or inferior. You are full of "can do" power. The same Spirit that raised Christ from the dead lives inside of you. Now, start putting things under your feet. God stated, "I have given you power to tread on all the power of the enemy." Think of that word *tread*. One definition says "to trample." If you will see these obstacles as being under your feet, as being already defeated, a new boldness will rise up. Your faith will activate God's power in a new way.

Turn Stumbling Blocks into
Stepping-Stones

I know a lady who was diagnosed with cancer. She's in her early thirties and has always been as healthy as can be. When she received the news, it was such a shock to her. Normally she's very outgoing and happy, but her whole personality changed. She became very depressed. All she thought about was how bad it was and how she might not make it. Instead of looking down at the cancer, she was looking up to it. She made it huge in her mind. The first place we lose the victory is in our own thinking. If you see the obstacle as being too big, it will keep you defeated.

That's why when David faced Goliath, even though Goliath was practically twice his size, was much stronger, and had more experience and more equipment, the first thing David said was, "I will defeat you and feed your head to the birds of the air." That's one of those enemies David looked down on. By faith, he saw it as being smaller. If David would have just looked at Goliath in the natural and thought about his size and inexperience, he would have never had the courage to face Goliath. David understood this principle. He knew how to see his enemies as being under his feet.

I told this young lady, "You have to change your perspective. Start looking down at that cancer. In the natural, it may be huge, but switch over to your eyes of faith. You and God are a majority. It was never meant to be a stumbling block. It was meant to be a stepping-stone. You have to shake off the self-pity, put on a new attitude, and declare as David did, 'Cancer, you will not defeat me. You are under my feet. I will fulfill my destiny. I will live out my days in good health. I am a victor and not a victim.'"

She changed her outlook. She got her fire back, her passion back.

She started fighting the good fight of faith. Today, she is four years cancer free and so happy. A couple of years ago she got married. The cancer wasn't a stumbling block. It ended up being a stepping-stone. But had she not seen the obstacle as being under her feet, I don't believe it would have turned out that way. If we let life overwhelm us, and we go around worried, stressed out, and locked in self-pity, we are not only affected mentally; we are also affected physically. The stress and worry weaken our immune system, which then can't fight off sickness and disease the way God created it to. The Scripture says, "The joy of the Lord is your strength." Joy is an emotion, and yet it creates something physical. It creates strength. When you're in tough times, you have to shake off the worry, shake off the

> *Joy is an emotion, and yet it creates something physical. It creates strength.*

self-pity, shake off the disappointment. Get your joy back. Have the right perspective. That enemy, that sickness, that obstacle—it's under your feet. It's not going to defeat you. It's going to promote you.

Armed with Strength

In II Samuel 22, it says, "You have armed me with strength for the battle. You have put my enemies under my feet." Friend, God knows every battle that you will ever face, including every temptation and every obstacle. He has not only put it under your feet, but He has armed you with strength for that battle. He has already equipped you. Quit telling yourself, "This is too much. I can't handle it." The greatest force in the universe is breathing in your direction. Tap into that power. Start declaring, "I am well able. I can do all things through Christ. I am strong in the Lord." When you do that, something is happening on the inside. You're getting stronger. Your immune system will work better. You'll have more energy. You'll make better decisions.

We've all been to the post office before and seen the signs on the wall of the "10 Most Wanted." Under their photos it sometimes says, "Armed and Dangerous." If the enemy had a post office, your picture would be up there. You are not a weakling. You are bad to the bone. You are a child of the Most High God. He has infused "can do" power into you. You have to start seeing yourself as being armed and dangerous.

> *You have to start seeing yourself as being armed and dangerous.*

When we get out of bed in the morning, the first thing we should do is power up. Get our minds going in the right direction. Remind yourself: "I'm ready for this day. I am equipped. I am empowered. I have my armor on. I have my shoes of peace. I'm not going to get upset. I'm not going to let people steal my joy. I'm not going to fight battles that aren't between me and my destiny. I have my helmet of salvation. I know I am forgiven. I am redeemed. I am approved by Almighty God. I've been handpicked by the Creator of the universe. I have my shield of faith. I'm expecting great things. I'm expecting to have an amazing year. I have my sword of the Spirit; I'm speaking God's Word. I know every enemy is under my feet. I've been armed with strength for this battle." What are we doing? Powering up, getting prepared for a blessed, victorious, faith-filled day.

You may be facing things that could easily steal your joy—a challenge in a relationship, a child not doing right, or an unfair situation at work. You could be stressed, uptight, and not sleeping at night. All through the day, especially when you're tempted to worry, you need to remind yourself: "This is under my feet. God is in control. It is not going to keep me from my destiny." Come back to that place of peace.

Stay in Peace, Use Your Footstool

Psalm 110 says, "God will make your enemies your footstool." What do you do with a footstool? You put your feet up on it. It indicates a position of rest. When we face difficulties, too often we take matters into our own hands. We get all worked up, thinking, *They did me wrong. I'm going to pay them back. I'm going to straighten them out.* Or our medical report is not good. We can't sleep at night. We're so uptight. So stressed out. But if you want God to make your enemy your footstool, you have to be still and know that He is God. When you're upset and trying to force things to happen, God is going to step back and let you do it on your own. It takes faith to say, "God, I know You are fighting my battles. I know You will make my wrongs right. You promised it would work out for my good. So I'm going to keep my joy and stay in peace."

When you put your feet up and rest, so to speak, God will take those things that seem as though they're over you, those things that are holding you back, and He will bring them under your feet. He will turn them around and make that enemy your footstool. When something is a footstool, you could say it serves you. It makes life easier. That's the way God is. When you stay in peace, God will take what's meant for harm and use it to your advantage.

Let's make it practical. Maybe at work this week or at the jobsite somebody is not treating you right. They're playing politics, not giving you the credit you deserve. Don't get upset. Just keep being your best each day. Stay on that high road. Your job is not to straighten people out. Your job is to stay in peace. When you're in peace, God is fighting your battles. When you're at rest, God will make your enemies your footstool.

> *Don't get upset. Just keep being your best each day. Stay on that high road.*

This is what happened with Joseph. He was betrayed by his brothers and sold into slavery, then falsely accused by Potiphar's wife and sent to prison for something that he didn't do. Joseph didn't get upset. He didn't try to pay people back. He didn't hold a grudge; he stayed in peace, stayed on the high road, and God turned it all around. The people who did Joseph wrong ended up working for him. His brothers, the same ones who betrayed him, came back and bowed low before him. Because he stayed in peace, God made his enemies his footstool.

Here's what I've learned. God can vindicate you better than you can vindicate yourself. If you will let God do it His way, it will be bigger, sweeter, more rewarding, and more honoring. God can take the very people who are trying to push you down, the people who are trying to make you look bad, and He can use them to promote you.

In the Scripture, Haman tried to push down Mordecai, who was Esther's cousin. He disrespected Mordecai, didn't give him the time of day, and tried to make him look bad. But one day the king told Haman to get a royal robe, put it on Mordecai, and march him up and down through the streets, announcing to everyone what a great man Mordecai was. Of all the people the king could have chosen to do that, it just so happened that he chose Haman to honor Mordecai, the very one who was trying to make him look bad. That's what happens when you let God do it His way. That boss at the office who's not giving you credit, don't worry about it. You're not working unto people. You're working unto God. God is keeping all the records. Perhaps instead of you working for that boss, one day that boss may be working for you. Stay in peace. God can make your enemies your footstool.

I have a friend who worked for a company for many years. He always gave it his best, but for some reason the owner of the company didn't like him. Even though the young man was bright and talented, the owner wouldn't take his opinion, wouldn't really give him the time of day. But as was true of Joseph, this young man didn't get bitter or try to prove to everyone who he was. He just stayed on the high road and kept being his best day after day. Eventually his boss fired him.

This young man went out and started his own real estate company and became extremely successful. He never thought much more about his former boss. He didn't have any ill will toward him at all. But God is a God of justice. He doesn't forget what you are owed. You may let it go, but God doesn't let it go. He is going to make sure you get exactly what you deserve.

Several years later, his former boss was downsizing the company and needed to move into a new building. It just so happened that the building the boss really wanted was owned by this young man. When he walked in and saw the young man he had fired and knew that he was the owner and had to negotiate with him, he nearly passed out. Now the former boss treated the younger man with the utmost respect. He listened to every word that he said. Today that former boss is paying rent to the young man he once fired. That's God bringing justice. That's God making your enemies your footstool.

There Is a Table Being Prepared for You

Stay in peace. God has your back. David said it this way in Psalm 23: "God will prepare a table before you in the presence of your enemies." That means God will not only make your wrongs right, but God will bless you in front of your enemies. God could promote you anywhere, but He will give you honor, recognition, and favor in front of the people who tried to pull you down. That person who lied about you and tried to keep you from rising higher, don't worry about him or her. One day they will see you receiving the credit that you deserve.

When people are talking about you or spreading gossip, just imagine that the angels are headed to the grocery store. God just turned the oven on. He is getting your dinner prepared. It's not going to be just you. There are going to be some onlookers. Those people who tried to push you down, they're watching you get promoted. They said you don't have what it takes. They're watching you accomplish your dreams. They wouldn't give you the time of day. Now they're trying to rent a facility from you. Stay in peace. God has you covered!

All the things that come against us to try to get us upset—people talking, gossiping, spreading rumors, not giving you respect—are all distractions. That's the enemy trying to lure us off course, get us bent out of shape, and waste our valuable time and energy on something that doesn't really matter. Don't give that the time of day. That's not a battle you're supposed to fight. Stay on the high road, and God will bring it under your feet. He will make those enemies your footstool.

When you're tempted to worry or tempted to get upset, just imagine yourself leaning back in a big comfortable chair, putting your feet up and resting them on top of that problem. You're saying, "God, it's under my feet. I know You are in control." When you're in peace, it's a position of power. When you're at rest, God is fighting your battles.

> *When you're in peace, it's a position of power.*

I know a man who was trying to get his wife to the United States. He is an American citizen, but his wife is not. She lives in Europe. He went to the government office to get a visa and the proper paperwork lined up. The man working behind the counter was very rude to him, wouldn't give him any help at all, and made it very confusing. Several weeks later this man had his paperwork filled out and notarized. He went back to the office, and the man was just as rude. The other authorities had told him it would probably take six months to get her visa, but this man said, "No, no. It's going to take at least *five years*.

We're all backed up. We're not going to get to your paperwork for a long time."

This man was very frustrated. He was even tempted to give the guy a piece of his mind. But instead he just kept his cool, reminded himself that it was under his feet. By faith, he could see God setting the dinner table. Several weeks later, he got a call back from the man at the office, telling him that the visa was ready. He was so shocked. It was a miracle. He went to the office and said to the man, "I thought you said it would be five years?"

The man said, "It should have been. But ever since I met you, I can't get you off my mind. I wake up thinking about you. I eat lunch thinking about you. I go to bed thinking about you. You're making my life miserable. Take the visa and go!" Friend, God knows how to apply pressure. God knows how to make somebody uncomfortable. You don't have to fight the battle. Stay on the high road and watch God make your enemies your footstool.

It Will Not Prosper Against You

Isaiah put it this way: "No weapon formed against you will prosper." He didn't say that we won't have difficulties or never have a problem. That's not reality. Challenges will come. People may talk. You may get a negative medical report. A family member may get off course. God said, "The problem may form, but you can stay in peace, knowing that it's not going to prosper against you." Because you're His child, because you're in the secret place of the Most High, God has a hedge of protection, mercy, and favor around you that the enemy cannot cross. No person, no sickness, no trouble, and no disability can stop God's plan for your life. All the forces of darkness cannot keep you from your destiny.

When you face these challenges and you're tempted to worry, you need to tell yourself: "This problem may have formed, but I have a promise from Almighty God that it is not going to prosper." In other words, "They may be talking about me, trying to make me look bad, but I'm not worried about it. I know God is my vindicator. He will take care of them." "My child may be running with the wrong crowd. That's all right. I know it's not permanent. It's temporary. As for me and my house, we will serve the Lord." "This medical report may not look good, but I know God made my body. He has me in the palm of His hand. Nothing can snatch me away."

I read about researchers who were studying Alzheimer's disease. They studied the brains of older people who had died, both people who'd had and not had the disease. They found that many people who had lesions on their brains that technically qualified them as having Alzheimer's had never shown any signs of it when they were alive. Their minds were clear. Their reasoning was good. Their memories were sharp. Scientifically they had Alzheimer's, but the symptoms never showed up. The common denominator is that they were positive. They were hopeful, and they stayed productive. That's what Isaiah said. Just because the problem forms doesn't mean it has to prosper. We may have things come against us because of genetics, things that have been passed down. The good news is God has the final say. God can override it, so stay in faith.

That's what happened with our friend Ramiro, who was born with no ears. The doctors told his parents, "He is never going to be able to hear or to speak." The problem had formed. In the natural, it didn't look good, but we serve a supernatural God. Ramiro has parents who believe it doesn't have to prosper. They didn't sit around in self-pity thinking, *Poor old us.* They knew they were armed with strength for that battle. They knew that situation was under their feet. They prayed. They believed. They declared God's favor.

When Ramiro was just a few months old, the doctors discovered that he had a very tiny start of an eardrum. These incredibly gifted doctors performed surgery, created new ears, and helped to correct the problem. Ramiro improved, had more surgeries, and continued to improve. Today, Ramiro can not only hear, not only speak, but he can also sing. He helps to lead worship for our young adults. You may have heard him on *American Idol* singing "Amazing Grace (My Chains Are Gone)" in front of millions of people.

Whatever you're facing, it is under your feet. It is not permanent. It's temporary. The power that is for you is greater than any power that comes against you. Keep the right perspective. You and God are a majority. You are armed and dangerous. The problem may have formed, but it is not going to prosper.

> *Whatever you're facing, it is under your feet. It is not permanent. It's temporary.*

Stay in the Place of Rest

Maybe you need to start putting things under your feet. You're letting that problem worry you and keep you up at night. God is saying, "I'll fight your battles, but you have to give them to Me." Come back to that place of peace. Don't let people or circumstances upset you. If somebody is not doing you right, let God be your vindicator. He knows how to make your wrongs right.

Remember, when you talk to that sickness, that obstacle, or that depression, as an act of faith, do as David did and look down. It's no match for you. If you will see these obstacles as being under your feet, God promises He will make your enemies your footstool. Instead of being a stumbling block, it will be a stepping-stone. As was true of Ramiro, nothing will keep you from your destiny. You will overcome every obstacle, defeat every enemy, and become everything God has created you to be.

I AM
PROSPEROUS

CHAPTER ELEVEN

Have an Abundant Mentality

God's dream for your life is that you would be blessed in such a way that you could be a blessing to others. David said, "My cup runs over." God is an overflow God. But here's the key: You can't go around thinking thoughts of lack, not enough, struggle, and expect to have abundance. If you've been under pressure for a long time and have difficulty making ends meet, it's easy to develop a limited mindset. *I'll never get out of this neighborhood.* Or, *I'll never have enough to send my kids to college.* That may be where you are now, but that's not where you have to stay.

God is called El Shaddai, the God of More Than Enough. Not the God of Barely Enough or the God of Just Help Me Make It Through. He's the God of Overflow. The God of Abundance.

Psalm 35 says, "Let them say continually, 'Let the Lord be magnified who takes pleasure in the prosperity of His children.'" They were supposed to go around constantly saying, "God takes pleasure in prospering me." It was to help them develop this abundant mentality. Your life is moving toward what you're constantly thinking about. If you're always thinking thoughts of lack, not enough, and struggle, you're moving toward the wrong things. All through the day, meditate on these thoughts: overflow, abundance, God takes pleasure in prospering me.

Barely Enough, Just Enough, and More Than Enough

In the Scripture, the Israelites had been in slavery for many years. That was the land of Barely Enough. They were just enduring, surviving, barely making it through. One day God brought them out of slavery and took them into the desert. That was the land of Just Enough. Their needs were supplied, but nothing extra. It says their clothes didn't wear out for forty years. I'm sure they were grateful. I don't know about you, but I don't particularly want to wear these same clothes for the next forty years. If I have to, I'm not going to complain, but that's not my idea of abundance. It wasn't God's either. God eventually took them into the Promised Land. That was the land of More Than Enough. The food and supplies were plenteous. The bundles of grapes were so large that two grown men had to carry them. It's called "the land flowing with milk and honey." *Flowing* means it didn't stop. It never ran out. It continued to have an abundance. That's where God is taking you.

You may be in the land of Barely Enough right now. You don't know how you're going to make it through next week. Don't worry. God hasn't forgotten about you. God clothes the lilies of the field. He feeds the birds of the air. He is going to take care of you.

You may be in the land of Just Enough. Your needs are supplied. You're grateful, but there's nothing extra, nothing to accomplish your dreams. God is saying, "I did not breathe My life into you to live in the land of Barely Enough. I didn't create you to live in the land of Just Enough." Those are seasons. Those are tests. But they are not permanent. Don't put your stakes down. You are passing through. It is only temporary. God has a Promised Land for you. He has a place of abundance, of more than enough, where it's flowing with provision, not just one time, but you'll continue to increase. You will continue to have plenty.

If you're in the land of Barely Enough, don't you dare settle there. That is where you are; it is not who you are. That is your location; it's not your identity. You are a child of the Most High God. No matter what it looks like, have this abundant mentality. Keep reminding yourself, "God takes pleasure in prospering me. I am the head and never the tail."

The Scripture says God will supply our needs "according to His riches." So often we look at our situations and think, *I'll never get ahead. Business is slow,* or *I'm in the projects. I'll never get out.* But it's not according to what you have; it's according to what He has. The good news is God owns it all. One touch of God's favor can blast you out of Barely Enough and put you into More Than Enough. God has ways to increase you beyond your normal income, beyond your salary, beyond what's predictable. Quit telling yourself, "This is all I'll ever have. Granddaddy was broke. Momma and Daddy didn't have anything. My dog is on welfare. My cat is homeless." Let go of all of that and have an abundant mentality.

> *"I am headed to overflow, to the land of More Than Enough."*

"This is not where I'm staying. I am blessed. I am prosperous. I am headed to overflow, to the land of More Than Enough."

Skinny Goat or Fatted Calf

I received a letter from a young couple. They had both been raised in low-income families. All they saw modeled growing up was lack, struggle, can't get ahead. Their families had accepted it, but not this couple. They had been coming to Lakewood and didn't have a not-enough mentality. They had an abundant mentality. They knew God had a Promised Land in store for them. They took a step of faith. On very average incomes, they decided to build their own house. They didn't take out a loan. Whenever they had extra funds, they would buy the materials and hire the contractors. A couple of years later, they moved into a beautiful house in a nice neighborhood, all debt free. It was as though God had multiplied their funds. Not long ago they sold that house for twice what they had put into it. The lady wrote, "We never dreamed we would be blessed like we are today." She went on to say, "My great-grandparents and my grandparents always told me that if I had beans and rice, that was good enough. But I always knew one day I would have steak."

If you're going to become everything God has created you to be, you have to make up your mind as she did. You are not going to settle for beans and rice. You are not going to get stuck in the land of Barely Enough or the land of Just Enough, but you're going to keep praying, believing, expecting, hoping, dreaming, working, and being faithful until you make it all the way into the land of More Than Enough. Now, there is nothing wrong with beans and rice. Nothing wrong with surviving. But God wants you to go further. God wants you to set a new standard for your family. He is an overflow God, a more-than-enough God.

Jesus told a parable about a prodigal son. This young man left home and blew all of his money, wasted his inheritance, and decided to return home. When his father saw him—the father represents God—he said to the staff, "Go kill the fatted calf. We're going to have a party."

But the older brother got upset. He said, "Dad, I've been with you this whole time, and you've never even given me a skinny goat."

Let me ask you. Do you have a fatted-calf mentality, or do you have a skinny-goat mentality? Do you think beans and rice are good enough, or do you say, "I want some enchiladas. I want some fajitas. I want some sopaipillas"? You can live on bread and water. You can survive in the land of Barely Enough. We can endure the land of Just Enough.

> *Do you think beans and rice are good enough?*

"Just enough to make it through. Just enough to pay my bills this week." But that is not God's best. Your Heavenly Father, the One who breathed life into you, is saying, "I have a fatted calf for you. I have a place for you in the land of More Than Enough."

Now don't go around thinking that you'll never get ahead. You'll never live in a nice place. You'll never have enough to accomplish your dreams. Get rid of that skinny-goat mentality and start having a fatted-calf mentality. God wants you to overflow with His goodness. He has ways to increase you that you've never dreamed.

> *Get rid of that skinny-goat mentality and start having a fatted-calf mentality.*

One Touch of God's Favor

I received a letter from a single mother. She immigrated to the United States from Europe many years ago. English is not her first language. She had three small children and didn't know how she would ever be able to afford to send them to college. It seemed as though she was at a disadvantage, living in a foreign country all alone, not knowing anybody.

She applied for a job as a secretary at a prestigious university. Several dozen other people applied for the same position. When she saw all the competition, she was tempted to feel intimidated. Negative thoughts were bombarding her mind. To make matters worse, the lady conducting the interview was harsh and condescending. But this mother didn't get frustrated. She didn't have an underdog mentality, thinking, *What's the use? I'm at a disadvantage. I'll never get ahead.* She had a fatted-calf mentality. She didn't see a way, but she knew God had a way.

All the applicants had to take a five-minute typing test. She was not a fast typist, but she started typing, doing her best. The bell went off signaling that her five minutes were up, so she stopped typing. But the lady in charge had gotten distracted answering a phone call and said to her gruffly, "Keep typing! That's not your bell." But it was her bell. It was right in front of her. She said, "Okay," and typed another five minutes. They added up the number of words she typed—ten minutes' worth—and divided it by five, and by far she had the best typing skills and ended up getting the job. One of the benefits of working for this university is that your children get to go to school for free. That was more than thirty years ago. Today, all three of her children have graduated from this very prestigious university, receiving more than seven hundred thousand dollars in education all free of charge.

One touch of God's favor can thrust you into more than enough. Don't talk yourself out of it. All through the day, say, "I am prosperous. I am coming into overflow. I will lend and not borrow."

A Place of Abundance

When the Israelites were in the desert in the land of Just Enough, they got tired of eating the same thing every day. They said, "Moses, we want some meat to eat out here." They were complaining, but at least for a little while they had a fatted-calf mentality.

Moses thought, *That's impossible. Meat out here in the desert? Steak for two million people?* There were no grocery stores, no warehouses to buy truckloads of meat. But God has ways to increase you that you've never thought of. God simply shifted the direction of the wind and caused a huge flock of quail to come into the camp. They didn't have to go after it. The food came to them. What's interesting is that quail don't normally travel that far away from the water. If there had not been a strong wind, the quail would have never made it way out there in the desert. What am I saying? God knows how to get your provision to you.

A statistician ran some numbers. Based on the size of the camp, the number of people, and enough quail to be three feet off the ground as the Scripture says, he concluded that there were approximately 105 million quail that came into the camp. That's an abundant God. He could have given them a couple of quail per person, which would have been four or five million quail. But God doesn't just want to meet your needs; He wants to do it in abundance. The question is, are you thinking skinny goat or are you thinking fatted calf?

"Well, Joel. I could never afford a nice place to live." Can I say this respectfully? Skinny goat.

"I could never send my kids to the college they really want to attend." Skinny goat.

"I could never build that orphanage. I could never support other families. I can barely support my own family."

Friend, God has a fatted calf, a place of abundance for you. He is not limited by your circumstances, by how you were raised, or by what you don't have. He is limited by what you're believing. Maybe you've had that skinny goat with you for years and years. You've become best friends. You need to announce to him today, "I'm sorry, but our relationship is over. It's done. We're going to be parting ways."

> *What limits you is what you're believing.*

He may cry and complain, "Baa-ah." He may ask, "Is there someone else?"

Tell him, "Yes, I've found a fatted calf. No more thinking not enough, barely enough, just enough. From now on I'm thinking more than enough; an abundant mentality."

Pressed Down and Running Over

When you live with this attitude, God will bless you in ways you've never imagined. I talked to a lady who has been through a lot of struggles. For years she was barely making it, but every Sunday she and her two sons would be here at Lakewood. In spite of all the obstacles, they didn't have a skinny-goat mentality. They were in the land of Barely Enough, but they didn't put their stakes down. They knew that wasn't their permanent address.

As this mother was, you have to be faithful in the wilderness if you're going to make it into the Promised Land. I'm not saying that everything is going to change overnight. There are going to be seasons of testing and proving. Thoughts are going to tell you, *It's never going to change*, but don't believe those lies. Keep being faithful right where you are, honoring God, thanking Him that you're coming into overflow.

This lady's son, from the time he was a little boy, always said that he was going to get a scholarship to go to college. He could have thought, *We're poor. I'm at a disadvantage.* But this mother taught her sons that God is a God of abundance. A while back, her son graduated number two in his high school. He received not one scholarship, not two, not seven. He was awarded nine scholarships, totaling more than 1.3 million dollars! His undergraduate, his master's, and his doctoral degrees are all paid for at Georgetown University. That's what happens when you say good-bye to the skinny goat and hello to the fatted calf.

Jesus talked about how when we give, it will be given back to us as good measure, pressed down, shaken together, and running over. What does that mean, *pressed down*?

I used to make chocolate chip cookies with our children. The recipe calls for three-fourths of a cup of brown sugar. When you pour the brown sugar in, it's so thick and dense, even when it hits the mark for three-fourths, you have to press it down. When you do, you can put in about twice what it looked like initially.

That's what God is saying. When you look full, you think you're blessed and healthy. All you need is one scholarship. You just want the house to sell for what you put into it. You just want quail for a day or two. God says, "That's fine, but I'm an overflow God. I'm a more-than-enough God. I'm about to press it down and make room for more of My increase. I'm going to press it down and show you My favor in a new way."

After He presses it down, He is going to shake it together and not just fill it to the top. He is going to take it one step further and give you so much that you're running over. You just wanted one scholarship. God says, "That's fine. I'm going to give you nine to make sure you're covered." You just wanted to get your money out of the house. God says, "I'm going to cause it to sell for double." You just wanted quail for a day or two. God says, "I'm going to give you steak for a whole month." That's the way our God is. Why don't you get in agreement and say, "God, I'm ready. I'm a giver. I have an abundant mentality. Lord, I want to thank You for good measure, pressed down, shaken together, and running over in my life."

Out of Lack into a Good and Spacious Land

A friend of mine has a son who got his driver's license a while back and really wanted a car. His father said to him, "Let's believe that God will give you a car." The son replied, "Dad, God is not going to give me a car. You can buy me a car." He said, "No, let's pray." They asked God to somehow make a way that he could have a car. A couple of months later, this man's employer called him in and said, "For the last two years, we've made a mistake on your paycheck. We've been underpaying you." They handed him a check for five hundred dollars more than the car they had been hoping to buy.

The Scripture says, "Is there anything too hard for the Lord?" There is no telling what God will do if you'll get rid of the skinny goat. God is about to press some things down. He is about to make room to show you His increase in a new way.

It says in the book of Exodus, "I am bringing you out of lack into a good and spacious land." Not a small land.

> "I am bringing you out of lack into a good and spacious land."

Not a little place. Tight. Crowded. Not enough room. Receive this into your spirit. God is bringing you into a spacious land. A land of more than enough. A land of plenty of room. A land that's flowing with increase, flowing with good breaks, flowing with opportunity, where you not only have enough for yourself, but you're running over. Running over with space. Running over with supplies. Running over with opportunity. If you're not in a good and spacious place, my challenge is, don't settle there. Don't let the skinny-goat mentality take root. Don't think beans and rice are good enough. That is not your permanent address. It's only temporary. God is taking you to a good and a spacious land.

"Well, Joel," you say, "are you one of those prosperity ministers?"

I don't like that term. That's somebody who talks only about finances. Prosperity to me is having your health. It's having peace in your mind. It's being able to sleep at night. Having good relationships. There are many things that money cannot buy. While I don't like the term *prosperity minister,* I must say I am not a poverty minister. I can't find a single verse in the Scripture that suggests we are supposed to drag around not having enough, not able to afford what we want, living off the leftovers, in the land of Not Enough. We were created to be the head and not the tail. Jesus came that we might live an abundant life. We represent Almighty God here on this earth. We should be examples of His goodness—so blessed, so prosperous, so generous, so full of joy—that other people want what we have.

If I brought my two children into your house and their clothes were all raggedy and worn out, with holes in their shoes, and their hair not combed, you would look at me and think, *What kind of father is he?* It would be a poor reflection on me. When you look good, dress well, live in a nice place, excel in your career, and are generous with others, that brings a smile to God's face. It brings Him pleasure to prosper you.

The Power to Get Wealth

My father was raised during the Great Depression. He grew up extremely poor and developed a poverty mindset. He was taught in seminary that you had to be poor to show God that you were holy. The church he pastored made sure he stayed holy by keeping him poor. He was making a little more than one hundred dollars a week, trying to raise his children, barely surviving. One time he and my mom kept a guest minister in their home all week. Sunday after the service, a businessman came up to my father and handed him a check for a thousand dollars. That's like five thousand dollars today. He said, "I want you to have this personally to help take care of the expenses of the guest minister." My father took the check by its corner as though it were contaminated. He said, "Oh, no, I could never receive this. We must put it in the church offering." He walked toward the offering plate, and with every step something said, "Don't do it. Receive God's blessings. Receive God's favor." He ignored it and dropped it in the offering plate. When he did, he said he felt sick to his stomach.

There is something inside us that says we're supposed to be blessed. We're supposed to live an abundant life. It's because we are children of the King. It was put there by our Creator. But here's the key: You have to give God permission to prosper you. You can't go around with a lack mentality, thinking, *I'll just take the leftovers to show everyone how humble I am. After all, God wouldn't want me to have too much. That would be greedy. That would be selfish.* Get rid of that false sense of humility. That's going to keep you from an abundant life.

> *There is something inside us that says we're supposed to be blessed.*

Consider these words from Deuteronomy 28 in *The Message* translation: "God will lavish you with good things. He will throw open the doors of His sky vaults and rain down favor. You will always be the top dog and never the bottom dog." You need to start seeing yourself as the top dog, not living off the leftovers, not able to afford what you want, in the land of Not Enough. Come over to the land of More Than Enough. It starts in your thinking. Give God permission to increase you. Give Him permission to lavish you with good things.

We think, *Is it wrong for me to want to live in a nice house or drive a nice car? Is it wrong to want funds to accomplish my dreams or wrong to want to leave an inheritance for my children?* God is saying, "It's not wrong. I take pleasure in prospering you." If it was wrong to have resources, abundance, and wealth, why would God have chosen to start the new covenant with Abraham? Abraham is called the father of our faith. The Scripture says, "Abraham was extremely rich in livestock and in silver and in gold." He was the Bill Gates of his day. God could have chosen anyone, but He chose Abraham—a man extremely blessed.

David left billions of dollars for his son to build the temple, and yet David is called "a man after God's own heart." Get rid of the thinking that *God wouldn't want me to have too much. That wouldn't be right. That might not look good.* It's just the opposite. When you look good, it makes God look good. When you're blessed, prosperous, and successful, it brings Him honor.

I realize that everything I have comes from God. Whether it is the suit that I'm wearing, my car, my house, or my resources, it's God's goodness. You don't have to apologize for what God has done in your life. Wear your blessings well.

The Scripture says, "It is the Lord who gives you power to get wealth." God wouldn't give you power to do something and then condemn you for doing it. There is nothing wrong with you having money. The key is to not let money have you. Don't let it become the focus of your life. Don't seek that provision. Seek the Provider. Money is simply a tool to accomplish your destiny and to advance His Kingdom.

A Thousand Times More

Victoria and I have big dreams in our hearts. It's going to take millions of dollars to do what's on the inside. These are dreams, not just for ourselves, for a bigger this or a bigger that, but a dream to build orphanages and a dream to build medical clinics. I can't do that with a limited, lacking, "God doesn't want me to have too much" mentality. I realize my Father owns it all. He makes streets out of gold. You are not going to bankrupt Heaven by believing for an abundant life. All God has to do is go pick up a chunk of pavement and give it to you. When you have this abundant mentality and a desire to advance the Kingdom, God will lavish you with good things. He will open up the doors of His sky vaults so that you not only accomplish your dreams, but you can help be a blessing to the world.

My prayer for you is found in Deuteronomy 1:11. It says, "May the Lord God of your fathers increase you a thousand times more than you are." Can you receive that into your spirit? A thousand times more favor. A thousand times more resources. A thousand times more income. Most of the time our thinking goes *TILT! TILT! TILT!* It's because we've been hanging out with that skinny goat too long. It's time to cut him loose. It's time to have a fatted-calf mentality. God is about to press some things down. He is about to make room for more of His increase. Now get up every morning and say, "Lord, I want to thank You that You are opening up Your sky vaults today, raining down favor, and lavishing me with good things. I am prosperous."

If you'll have this abundant mentality, I believe and declare you won't live in the land of Just Enough or the land of Barely Enough, but you're coming into the land of More Than Enough.

I AM
FOCUSED

CHAPTER TWELVE

Redeem the Time

Time is one of the most valuable commodities that we have. It's more valuable than money. You can make more money, but you can't make more time. The Scripture tells us to redeem the time. That means don't waste it. Don't live this day unfocused, undisciplined, and unmotivated. We have a responsibility to use our time wisely. We're not always going to be here. This day is a gift. Are you living it to the fullest? With purpose and passion? Pursuing your dreams? Or are you distracted? Indifferent? Just doing whatever comes along? Are you in a job you don't like? Hanging out with people who are pulling you down? That's not redeeming the time; that's wasting the time. Just like you spend money, you are spending your life. You're either investing it or you're wasting it.

The first step is to set goals: short-term goals and long-term goals. What do you want to accomplish this week? Where do you want to be five years from now? Do you have a plan? Are you taking steps to get there? Don't go another three years on a job you don't like, doing something that you're not passionate about. Life is flying by. This is your one shot. You don't get a do-over. We can't relive our twenties or thirties. Once this day is over, we can never get it back.

Paul said in Ephesians, "Make the most of every opportunity. Don't be vague and thoughtless, but live purposefully and accurately." If you're going to reach your highest potential, you have to be an "on purpose" person. You know where you're going. You're

> *"Make the most of every opportunity."*

not vague, distracted, waiting to see what happens. You're focused. You're making the most of each opportunity. Let me put it in more practical terms: Staying on social media for hours a day and catching up on the latest gossip is not redeeming the time. Playing video games for hours a day when you could be studying is not redeeming the time. Talking on the phone for hours a day to a friend who's not going anywhere and has no dreams is not redeeming the time.

God has given you a present. It's called "today." What are you going to do with it? This is a call to action. Get focused. Get organized. Set your goals. Make your plans. God could have chosen anyone to be here, but He chose you.

Live a Well-Spent Life

The Scripture talks about living well-spent lives. When we go to bed at night, we should ask ourselves, "Did I live a well-spent day? Did I take steps toward my goals? Was I a blessing to someone else? Did I invest my time or did I waste my time?" I read that the average person spends more than eighty hours a year looking for things they misplaced—car keys, cell phones, glasses, receipts, and children! Somebody said that the reason God gives babies to young people is because older people would forget where they left them. Do yourself a favor—save yourself eighty hours a year and get organized. Redeem that time.

I know too many people who are incredibly talented and have great potential, but they're not disciplined when it comes to how they spend their time. They have good intentions, but they're easily distracted and end up off course. There are a thousand good things you can give your time to each day. You have to be disciplined to stay focused on what's best for you. If not, you'll end up chasing the latest trend, trying to keep up with your friends, distracted, entangled in things that are not a part of your destiny.

I heard about a man who was walking through the airport on the way to his flight. He saw a sign on the terminal wall that said, KNOW YOUR FUTURE, 25 CENTS. He was intrigued by it, so he walked over and put a quarter in the slot. The computer readout said, "Your name is John Smith. You're on the 2:20 flight to Boston." He couldn't believe it. He thought, *How does this thing know my name? How does it know my flight number?* A friend was walking by, so he called him over and said, "Look at this." He put in another quarter. It did it again. "Your name is John Smith. You're on the 2:20 flight to Boston." His friend looked kind of puzzled, shrugged his shoulders, and went on. The man reached in his pocket to get another quarter out and try it again, but he didn't have any more coins. He had to walk way back to the newsstand to get change. There was a long line, and he waited and waited. He finally got a quarter, came back, and put it in the slot. It said, "Your name is John Smith. You just *missed* the 2:20 flight to Boston."

Stay focused. It's easy to get sidetracked by things that pull you off course, and when you finally look up, the day is gone, or the year is gone, or twenty years have gone. Nothing will be sadder than to come to the end of life and think, *Why did I waste so many days? Why didn't I live focused?* Make this decision with me

> *Make this decision with me that you're going to redeem the time.*

that you're going to redeem the time. We have a responsibility. God has entrusted you with His life. He breathed His breath into you. He's put gifts and talents inside you. You have seeds of greatness. You're not just on planet Earth taking up space. You're a person of destiny. With that gift of life comes a responsibility to develop your talents, to pursue your dreams, and to become who God's created you to be.

Make Sure You Are Running with Purpose

On a regular basis, you need to reevaluate what you're doing. Refocus your life. Get rid of any distractions. Paul said in another place, "I run with purpose in every step." When we understand the value of time and see each day as the gift that it is, it helps us to keep the right perspective. You realize every battle is not worth fighting. You don't have time to get engaged in conflicts that are not between you and your God-given destiny. If somebody has a problem with you, as long as you're being your best, doing what God's put in your heart, with all due respect, that's their problem and not yours. You don't have to resolve conflicts with every person. Some people don't want to be at peace with you. That's a distraction. Don't waste your valuable time fighting battles that don't matter.

When you realize your days are numbered, you don't respond to every critic. You don't try to convince people to like you who are never going to like you. You accept the fact that some people are never going to give you their approval. But that's okay. You know you have Almighty God's approval. When you're redeeming the time, you're not trying to keep someone happy who's never going to be happy. With some people, no matter what you do for them, it's not going to be enough. But their happiness is not your responsibility. Always be kind and respectful, but your attitude should be, *If you don't want to be happy, that's fine, but you're not going to keep me from being happy. I know this day is a gift, and I'm not going to live it trying to change things that I cannot change or trying to fix people who don't want to be fixed.* That's redeeming the time.

When you realize your time is limited, you don't get offended. You don't get upset because somebody's playing politics; you don't get stressed out because somebody's trying to make you look bad. You let it go and trust God to make your wrongs right.

A lady was telling me about a family member who had done her wrong. She was very negative and starting to get bitter. I told her what I'm telling you. Life is too short to live that way. Let it go, and God will be your vindicator. She didn't want to hear it. She said, "No, I'm not going to be happy until he apologizes." What she doesn't realize is that she is wasting valuable days. He may never apologize. I wonder how many days that we've wasted doing similar things. We can't say that we redeemed the time; we didn't appreciate the day. We just dragged through it being upset, offended, and discouraged.

The Scripture says, "Don't let the sun go down on your anger." The reason many people have no joy or enthusiasm is because they go to bed each night with unforgiveness in their heart. They're reliving their hurts, thinking about their disappointments. Here's the problem: If

> *"Don't let the sun go down on your anger."*

the sun goes down with bitterness, it will come back up with bitterness. If it goes down with resentment, it comes back up with resentment. That's blocking God's blessings. It's keeping you from seeing the bright future. If you want the sun to shine brightly in your life once again, before you go to bed each night, you need to say, "God, I'm releasing every negative thing that's happened to me today. I'm releasing every hurt, releasing every worry, releasing every disappointment. I'm forgiving the people who did me wrong. God, I'm going to bed in peace." When you do that, the sun will go down with nothing blocking it. When it comes back up the next morning, you'll have a new spring in your step, you'll be excited about the day and ready for your future. Don't go to bed at night with any kind of defeat still in your mind.

Invest Your Time Wisely

I talked to a young lady who's a television reporter at a local station in Houston, and during Hurricane Ike, she was out covering the story. Her assignment was to find people who were down and out and having a hard time finding food because of the hurricane. She was at one of the food drops, talking to people in line, but nobody had a sad story. They were all grateful that they were alive and talking about how they were going to make it. Victoria and I and some Lakewood volunteers happened to be there. She came over with the camera and asked me, "What's the worst thing that you've seen?" I said, "Yes, some people are struggling, but they have faith; they're overcomers. They know they're victors and not victims." She thought, *Well, I knew Joel wasn't going to tell me anything sad.* So she went and found Victoria, who was worse than me. She said, "These people are fired up. They know God's in control, and something better is coming their way."

When the reporter got back to the station, she told her supervisor, "I couldn't find any sad stories, but I got Joel and Victoria Osteen to comment on the hurricane." She thought they would be excited, but it was just the opposite. They didn't want us; they wanted sad stories. She ended up getting terminated over that incident. They let her go! She could have been discouraged, depressed, and bitter, but she understands this principle that every day is a gift from God. She started thanking God that new doors were going to open and thanking Him that favor was coming her way. Not long after that, she received a phone call from a very prestigious broadcasting company. They saw her report on the hurricane—the same one that got her fired. They said, "We'd like to offer you a full-time position to come and head up the department that does all of our documentaries." That was a dream come true. She couldn't believe it. She gave me a big hug and said, "Joel, I want to thank you and Victoria for getting me fired."

I've heard it said, "Disappointments are inevitable, but misery is optional." No matter what kind of setbacks you face, no matter who does you wrong, you don't have to drag through life defeated, depressed, and bitter. Start redeeming the time. Do as she did. Start thanking God that He's in control. Thank Him that new doors are opening. Thank Him that favor is coming your way. The truth is that we all go through the valleys, but the valleys are what lead us to higher mountains. They're not permanent; they're only temporary. Here's a key: When you're in the valley, instead of sitting around thinking about your problems, go out and do something good for somebody else. Volunteer

> *We all go through the valleys, but the valleys are what lead us to higher mountains.*

while you're in the valley. Usher while you're in the valley. Cheer somebody up while you're in the valley. Mow somebody's lawn while you're in the valley. When you invest your time the right way in helping others, those seeds that you sow will create the harvest you need, not to just get out of the valley, but to come to a higher mountain, to come up to a new level of your destiny.

Reevaluate Who You Spend Your Time With

It's not only important how we spend our time, but with whom we spend it. To redeem the time may mean you have to prune off some relationships that are not adding value to your life. Don't hang around people who are not going anywhere, who have no goals or dreams. People who are not focused and not disciplined. They compromise and take the easy way out. If you tolerate mediocrity, it will rub off on you. If you hang out with jealous, critical, unhappy people, you will end up jealous, critical, and unhappy. That's what it says in Proverbs: When you walk with wise men, you will become wise.

Take a look at your friends. That's what you're going to be like in a few years. If your friends are winners, leaders, givers, and successful, if they have integrity and a spirit of excellence and are positive and motivated, then those good qualities are going to rub off on you. When you're with them, you're investing your time. They're making you better. But if you hang out with people who are sloppy, undisciplined, unmotivated, and not going anywhere, let me give you some great advice: Find some new friends. You cannot become who God created you to be hanging out with them. They may be good people, and they may have good hearts, but your destiny is too great, your assignment is too important, and your time is too valuable to let them drag you down.

The only thing that's keeping some people from a new level of their destiny is wrong friendships.

The only thing that's keeping some people from a new level of their destiny is wrong friendships. You cannot hang out with chickens and expect to soar like an eagle. You don't have to make some big announcement and go 'tell them, "Hey, man, I'm cutting you off. Joel said to get rid of you." No, do me a favor and leave my name out of this. But you can just gradually spend less and less time with them. "Well, what if I hurt their feelings?" Well, what if they keep you from your destiny?

. I heard about a lady who was reevaluating her friendships. Her answering machine said, "I'm sorry I missed your call. I'm making some changes in my life. If I don't call you back, please know you were one of those changes." I'm thinking about all the people who haven't called me back!

But here's the key: If you don't let go of the wrong people, you'll never meet the right people. Sometimes we can outgrow a friendship. It was good at one time. For a few years, you were fulfilled. But now you've grown more than they have. You're running at a different pace. Your gifts are coming out in a greater way. That doesn't make them a bad person. It's just a new season. Human nature likes to hold on to the old. We like to keep everything the same. But the truth is that it's healthy for seasons to change. It doesn't mean you can't still be their friend; you just know you cannot spend as much time with them and become all you were created to be.

> *If you don't let go of the wrong people, you'll never meet the right people.*

There are people who come into our lives who are like scaffolding. They're designed to be there for a period of time. And I'm not talking about a marriage situation; I'm talking about friendships. These people help us grow, inspire us, and motivate us. But like that scaffolding, at some point, it's got to come off the building. If the scaffolding stayed up, the building would never be what it was meant to be. Appreciate the people who have helped you. Always honor them, but be big enough to recognize when their part in your story is over. On a regular basis, you need to reevaluate your friendships and the people with whom you choose to spend time. Are they in the right position? Has the position changed? Could it be that it's a new season?

Be Careful Who You Allow into Your Inner Circle

When Jesus was on the earth, He was very selective with His friendships. Everyone wanted to be close to Him. But He chose only twelve disciples with whom to spend most of His time. Out of those twelve, three were His close friends: Peter, James, and John. One could be considered His best friend, John. He was described as the disciple whom Jesus loved. You may know a lot of people and have many acquaintances, but you have to be careful who you allow into your inner circle. You can't have twenty best friends. The higher you go and the more successful you are, the tighter your circle needs to become. You may have twenty people you call friends, and that's great. But make sure the two or three you choose to be close to you are 100 percent for you. Make sure they believe in you, stick up for you, and are with you through thick or thin. It could be that you're not seeing God's best because your team is weak. You're investing valuable time in people who were never supposed to be a part of your inner circle. If your team is weak, you're going to be weak.

In Mark 5, Jesus was traveling to another city to pray for a little girl who had died. When He arrived at the home, the Scripture states that Jesus didn't allow anyone to go in with Him except for Peter, James, and John. His inner circle. Why? Jesus knew when He got in that room where the little girl was lying dead, He needed people who wouldn't question who He was. He needed people who wouldn't ask, "Are you sure you're the Son of God? What if she doesn't get healed? Do you have a backup plan?"

When you're in the heat of the battle, when you need God's favor, when you need a breakthrough, when you need a legal situation to turn around, you cannot afford to have people in your inner circle asking, "Do you really think you're going to get well? My grandmother died of that same thing. Do you really think you're going to get out of debt? Business is so slow." You need people who are joined in spirit with you. You need people who will say, "If you're bold enough to believe it, count on me. I'm bold enough to agree with you." "If you believe you can break that addiction, I'm not going to tell you ten reasons why you can't. My report is you are well able." "If you believe you can get your degree, or you can start that business, or you can see your marriage restored, then count on me. I'm on board. I'm all for you."

You need people who will join faith with you and not try to talk you out of what's in your heart. Jesus got to the home, and everyone was so distraught. You can imagine the crying, weeping, and sorrow. Jesus looked at them and said, "Don't be upset. She's not dead; she's only asleep." Their sorrow turned to mocking, ridiculing, and making fun. "What do you mean she's not dead? Of course, she's dead." What Jesus did next is very significant. It's a key to living in victory. The Scripture says they "mocked and jeered at Him, and Jesus put them out." Notice that the Son of God asked them to leave. He showed them the door. Jesus knew the importance of having people around Him who understood His destiny. His attitude was, *I don't need your doubt. I don't need you telling Me what I can't do. I'm going to surround Myself with believers, with people of faith, with people who understand My assignment.*

If you have people close to you who are constantly pulling you down, telling you what you can't do and how you'll never accomplish your dreams, understand that it is scriptural to show them the door. It may be difficult, but you have to have the attitude, *I cannot fulfill my destiny with your critical spirit in my life. I can't become who*

*I was created to be with you dragging me down. I love you, but I can't
allow you in my inner circle. I'm going to love you from a distance.*

This is what Jesus did. He took only the girl's parents and Peter,
James, and John into the little girl's room. He spoke to that girl, and
she came back to life. Think of this. Jesus could have healed her in
front of the whole laughing, mocking, ridiculing crowd. He's God,
and He can do anything. But He was showing us this principle: Who
you have in your inner circle is extremely important. If Jesus went
to the trouble to ask the wrong people to leave, if He took the time
to weed out the doubters, the naysayers, and the people who didn't
believe in Him, if He was that concerned about His inner circle, how
much more concerned should we be with who's in our inner circle?

Pay attention to who's on your team. Who's speaking into your life?
To whom are you giving your time and attention? In practical terms,
who are you eating lunch with every
day at the office? Who are you talking to on the phone so much? Are they
building you up or tearing you down?
Are they pushing you toward your des-
tiny, or are they telling you what you can't do? Are they modeling
excellence, integrity, character, and godliness, or are they lazy, sloppy,
and undisciplined? You have a responsibility to redeem your time.

> Pay attention to who's on
> your team. Who's speak-
> ing into your life?

Don't waste it with people who don't sharpen you. If you don't
politely show them the door, they can keep you from your destiny.
Sometimes we know a person's not good for us and we know they're
dragging us down, but we think if we let them go, we're going to be
lonely. Yes, you may be lonely for a season, but you'll never give up
something for God without Him giving you something better back
in return. God will not only give you new friends, He'll give you
better friends. People who inspire you, people who celebrate you,
and people who push you forward.

This may mean that you have to change whom you eat lunch with at the office every day. That person who's always finding fault, critical, and bad-mouthing the boss, you don't need that poison in your life. That's not redeeming the time. You may have to change hanging out with that neighbor who's always depressed, defeated, and has a sad song. If you stay there, you're going to end up defeated. It's better to make the change and be lonely for a season than to be poisoned for a lifetime.

Don't Waste Another Day

When we come to the end of our days, God is going to ask us, "What did you do with the time I entrusted to you? Did you develop your gifts and talents? Did you accomplish your assignment? How did you spend your life?" It's not going to be a good excuse to say, "God, I got distracted, but my friend got me off course." "God, I lived bitter, but somebody did me wrong." "God, I was negative, but my company let me go." I'm asking you to quit making excuses and start redeeming the time. We're not always going to be here. The Scripture says, "Our life is like a mist. We're here for a moment, then we're gone."

Make this decision that you're going to be an on-purpose person. Set your goals and be disciplined to stick with it. Don't waste any more days. Prune off those relationships that are not adding to your life. And don't go to bed with any kind of defeat, bitterness, or negativity still in your mind. This day is a gift. Make sure you're investing your time and not wasting it. If you do this, the seeds of greatness inside you are going to take root and begin to flourish. You're going to see God's favor in new ways.

I AM
DETERMINED

CHAPTER THIRTEEN

Finishing Grace

It doesn't take a lot of effort to start things—a diet, school, a family. Starting is easy. Finishing is what can be difficult. Almost any young lady can have a baby, but it takes a mother to really raise that child. Any two people can get married, but it takes commitment to stick with it for the long haul. Anyone can have a dream, but it takes determination, perseverance, and a made-up mind to see it come to pass. The question is not "Will you start?" but "Will you finish?" Will you finish the diet? Will you finish school? Will you finish raising your children? Too many people start off well. They have big dreams. They're excited about their futures. But along the way they have some setbacks. It's taking longer than they thought. Somebody didn't do what they said. Over time, they get discouraged and think, *What's the use? It's never going to work out.*

But God is called "the author and the finisher of our faith." He has not only given you the grace to start; He has given you the grace to finish. When you are tempted to get discouraged, give up on a dream, give up on a relationship, or give up on a project, you have to remind yourself, *I was not created to give up. I was not created to quit. I was created to finish.*

You have to shake off the discouragement. Shake off the self-pity. Shake off what somebody said. If you will keep moving forward in faith, honoring God, you will come into a strength that you didn't have before, a force pushing you forward. That's finishing grace. That's God breathing in your direction, helping you to become who He created you to be.

This grace is available, but you have to tap into it. It's not going to do us any good if we sit around in self-pity, thinking about how difficult things are, what didn't work out. "Well, my college professor is so hard. I'll never pass his course."

Friend, you have the grace to finish. Quit talking defeat and start talking victory. "I can do all things through Christ. I am full of wisdom, talent, and creativity. I will pass this course." When you say that, finishing grace will help you do what you could not do on your own.

Even in simple things. You start cleaning your house. Five minutes later, you think, *I don't feel like doing this. I am so tired. This is so boring.* Instead, turn it around and tell yourself, "I am strong in the Lord. I am full of energy. I am healthy. This is no match for me." If you will tap into this finishing grace, you will vacuum your house as though you're on a mission from God—vacuuming up dirt, coins, socks, children, anything else that gets in your way!

> *Finishing grace is available, but you have to tap into it.*

"He Will Bring You to a Flourishing Finish"

Maybe you're tempted to give up on a dream. Things haven't turned out the way you planned. It was going fine at first, but then you had some obstacles and you think, *It just wasn't meant to be.* Here's what I've learned. The enemy doesn't try to stop you from starting. He has seen a lot of people start. That doesn't bother him. But when you have a made-up mind and keep pushing forward, doing the right thing, taking new ground, when he sees you getting closer, he will work overtime to try to keep you from finishing. Don't get discouraged when you have setbacks, people come against you, or you get a negative medical report. That's a sign that you're moving toward your finish line.

The enemy was fine when you got started. He was fine when you were far from finishing. No big deal. But when you began to make progress, that got his attention. That's when he threw out some obstacles, some challenges. Where you confused him is he thought you would give up after the first few difficulties. He thought you would get discouraged when that friend turned on you, when you lost that client, when your child got in trouble, but instead you kept moving forward, thanking God that He is in control, thanking Him that He is fighting your battles, thanking Him that no weapon formed against you will prosper. What were you doing? Tapping into finishing grace. When you should have gotten weaker, you got stronger. When you should have been depressed, you had a smile on your face. When you should have been complaining, you had a song of praise. Instead of talking about how big the problem was, you were always talking about how big your God is. When you should have gone under, God caused you to go over. When you didn't see a way, He made a way. When people came against you, He fought your battles and you came out better than you were before.

You may be up against challenges right now. It's because you are moving forward. You're making progress. Keep reminding yourself that God is the author and the finisher of your faith. He helped you to get started. That's great, but there's something more important: He is going to help you finish. He didn't bring you this far to leave you.

It says in Philippians, "God began a good work in you, and He

> *You are coming to a flourishing finish, a finish more rewarding than you ever imagined.*

will continue to perform it until it is complete." One translation says, "He will bring you to a flourishing finish"—not a defeated finish, where you barely make it and are beat up and broke. You are coming to a flourishing finish, a finish more rewarding than you ever imagined.

Be in It to Win It

When Joseph was a teenager, God gave him a dream that one day he would rule a nation. His father, Jacob, loved him very much. Everything started off great for Joseph. He had a big dream, a supportive family. Life was good. But when Joseph was seventeen, things started to go wrong. His brothers became jealous of him and turned on him. They threw him into a pit and left him there to die. Eventually they changed their minds and sold him into slavery. He was taken to Egypt and resold to a man named Potiphar. Joseph hadn't really done anything wrong, yet his whole world had been turned upside down. It looked as if his dream was dead; he had been betrayed by his family and enslaved in a foreign country. If that wasn't bad enough, they put him in prison for years for something that he didn't do.

Joseph must have been depressed, angry, bitter, and upset. Nothing had turned out right. But Joseph understood this principle. He knew he had the grace not only to start but to finish what God put in his heart. He knew the enemy wouldn't be fighting him if he wasn't heading toward his destiny. So he stayed in faith. He kept doing the right thing when the wrong thing was happening. He was not working unto people but working unto God.

One day the Pharaoh, the leader of the nation, had a dream that he didn't understand. Joseph was able to interpret the dream. Pharaoh was so impressed with Joseph that he brought him out of prison and put him in charge of the whole nation. Joseph's dream came to pass.

God has put something on you that will override people being against you. It will override bad breaks and injustice. You have the grace not just to start. You have something even more powerful—the grace to finish. When you have an attitude like Joseph had, you cannot stay defeated. Life may push you down, but God will pull you back up. People may do you wrong, but God will be your vindicator. Situations may look impossible, but God can do the impossible. When you have finishing grace, all the forces of darkness cannot stop you. You may suffer some setbacks, bad breaks, and injustice. But don't worry. It's only temporary. It's just a detour on the way to your destiny. That's a sign that you are moving toward your finish line.

The enemy doesn't fight people who are going the wrong way, people who are off course, discouraged, distracted, bitter, and angry. That's where he wants you. He comes against people who are headed toward the fullness of their destinies, people who are taking new ground, people like you who are coming into a flourishing finish. Our attitude should be, *I have a made-up mind. I am determined. I'm going to keep moving forward in spite of the bad break, in spite of the loss, in spite of the negative report, in spite of the critics. My destiny is too great and my assignment is too important to get discouraged, distracted, and bitter. I'm not going halfway or three-fourths of the way. I'm going to become all God has created me to be.*

When you're tempted to get discouraged and settle, it's because you're close to your breakthrough. You're close to seeing the problem turn around. You're close to meeting the right person. Pharaoh is about to call you, so to speak.

> *When you're tempted to get discouraged and settle, it's because you're close to your breakthrough.*

The good break is on the way. The healing is on the way. The contract is on the way. Now you have to tap into this finishing grace. Friend, you've come too far to stop now. You've believed too long. You've worked too hard. You've invested too much. It may be difficult. Negative voices may be telling you, "It's never going to work out. Forget it. Just settle where you are." But don't believe those lies. You are close to your destiny.

When the going gets tough, you have to dig your heels in and say, "I am in it to win it. I am not moved by this opposition. I am not moved by what I see or by what I feel. I'm moved by what I know, and I know this: I have the grace to finish. I know this: God began a good work in me, and He is going to complete it. So I'm going to keep honoring God. I'm going to keep being good to people. I'm going to keep on being my best." Every day you do that, you are passing the test. You are one day closer to coming into your finish line.

Strength in Reserve

The Scripture says, "As your days are, so shall your strength be." This means your strength will always be equivalent to what you need. If you were to get a negative medical report, you're going to have the strength to deal with it. You're not going to fall apart. "Oh, I can't believe this is happening." Your strength will always match what you're up against.

When my father went to be with the Lord, my first thought was, *How am I going to deal with this?* My dad and I were very close. We had traveled the world together. All of a sudden he was gone. But what I thought would be very devastating and would knock the wind out of me wasn't anything like I had imagined. I felt a peace I had never felt, a strength, a resolve, a determination. I should have been upset and anxious, but that whole time I was at peace. Deep down I felt a rest. In my mind there were thoughts of worry, anxiety, and discouragement, but in my spirit I could hear God whispering, "Joel, I'm in control. It's all going to work out. I have you in the palm of My hand." That was finishing grace pushing me forward, propelling me into my destiny.

The psalmist said in Psalm 46, "God is a very present help in times of need." In the difficulties of life, if you will get quiet and turn off the negative voices, you will feel a peace that passes understanding. You should be falling apart, but there is grace for every season.

Victoria and I were in Colorado one time, driving through the mountains. We rented a large SUV with an eight-cylinder engine. As long as we were on the flat roads, the engine was as quiet as could be. But as we started going up the steep winding mountain roads, just when we thought the vehicle couldn't make it, when it looked like it was going to stop, you could hear those extra two cylinders kick in. You could actually feel the car, almost as though it lifted up and took off with a new power.

Those two extra cylinders were there all the time. The extra power was always available. It just showed up when we needed it. It was strength in reserve. Sometimes in life we think, *How am I going to make it up that steep hill? I've gotten this far, but how am I going to deal with this illness? How am I going to raise this difficult child? I went through a loss, and I don't think I can go on.* The good news is that God has some strength in reserve for you. When you hit a tough time, don't worry. There are two more cylinders about to kick in, a strength you haven't tapped into yet. You're going to feel a force pushing you forward, taking you where you could not go on your own. That's finishing grace.

I've learned that the closer you get to your destiny, the tougher the battles become. The higher you go up the mountain, the more

God promotes you, and the steeper the hill is. The critics will come out of the woodwork. People may not celebrate you. There will be unexpected challenges—a health issue, a business slows down, or you lose a loved one. It's easy to think, *I was doing so well. If I just wouldn't have had this bad break. Now I've got this steep hill to climb.* That challenge is a sign that you are close to your destiny. The same God who gave you the grace to start is the same God who is going to help you finish. He knows exactly where your path is leading. Nothing you're facing is a surprise to Him. He knows every hill, every disappointment, and every setback. He said that His grace is sufficient. You will never come to a hill where you don't have the strength to climb it.

You may face some challenges, as I did when my dad went to be with the Lord, when you think, *I don't know how I'm going to make it up this hill.* The reason you think that way is you haven't needed those two extra cylinders yet. You have not felt the full force of finishing grace. When it kicks in, it's going to propel you forward. You're going to climb mountains that you thought were way too steep. You're going to overcome obstacles that looked insurmountable, accomplish dreams that you thought were impossible. How will you do this? Finishing grace. You'll tap into strength in reserve.

> *You're going to overcome obstacles that looked insurmountable, accomplish dreams that you thought were impossible.*

Guard Your Fire

This is what the Apostle Paul did in the Scripture. He faced some huge hills. It didn't look as though he could fulfill his destiny. He was doing the right thing, sharing the good news, helping other people, but then he was arrested and put in prison. The closer he got to his destiny, the more obstacles he faced. He was alone, in a dungeon, on death row. It looked as though God had forgotten about him. But Paul wasn't defeated, depressed, or feeling sorry for himself. Even though he was in chains, he couldn't be stopped from doing what God wanted him to do. Since Paul couldn't go out and speak publically, he thought, *No problem. I'll start writing.* He wrote book after book. "Here's a letter to the Ephesians. Here's a letter to the Colossians, to the Romans, to the Corinthians." He wrote over half of the books of the New Testament, much of it from a prison cell. His enemies thought they were stopping him, but they were doing just the opposite: causing his voice to become amplified. Here we are some two thousand years later, and we still feel Paul's influence. What they meant for harm, God used for good.

People may try to stop you, but finishing grace will get you to where you're supposed to be. They may push you down, but finishing grace will lift you back up. They may try to discredit, belittle, or leave you out. Don't get upset. They are a part of the plan to get you to your destiny. God will use them to propel you forward. As long as you stay in faith and keep honoring God, you will accomplish your assignment. He is the author and the finisher of your faith.

Now, quit focusing on who is against you, on how steep the hill is, on how impossible it looks. God has the final say. He brought Joseph out of prison. Paul stayed in prison, but they both fulfilled their destinies. If God doesn't turn it around the way you thought, He may cause you to have great influence right in the midst of your enemies as Paul did. In the midst of those difficulties, you can shine, be a bright light, and have God's favor. Bottom line is this: No person can stand against our God. No bad break can keep you from your destiny. God has given you finishing grace. He is going to get you to where you're supposed to be.

When Paul came to the end of his life, he said, "I have finished my course." One translation says, "I finished my course with joy." Notice, he didn't finish defeated, depressed, or sour. He finished with a smile on his face. He finished with a spring in his step. He finished with a song in his heart. That's what it means to have a flourishing finish.

We all have things come against us. It's easy to lose our passion and drag through life discouraged, negative, and bitter, but there is no victory if you finish your course that way. You have to make up your mind, *I'm not only going to finish my course; I'm going to finish it with joy, with a good attitude. Not complaining, but with a song of praise. Not thinking about what I don't have, but thanking God for what I do have. Not looking at what's wrong in my life, but thanking God for what's right in my life.* When you tap into finishing grace, you won't drag through the day. You will enjoy the day.

Thousands of years ago in Greece, there was a famous race called the Torch Relay. All of the runners received a torch. At the start of the race, they would light their torches, and the runners would take off running with their torches lit. The only way you could win the race was to cross the finish line with your torch still lit. Even if you finished first, if your fire went out, you were disqualified. So the whole time they were running, in the forefront of their minds was protecting their fire, keeping it from wind or rain or anything that might put it out. They were constantly checking their torches to make sure that they were still lit.

It's the same principle in the race of life. If you're going to finish your course with joy, you have to guard your fire. You can't let your flame go out. Too many people have lost their passion. They're still running, but their torch is no longer lit. At one time they were passionate about their dreams, then they had some setbacks. Now they're running, which is good, but they let their fire go out. They lost their zeal. If that's you, I've come to relight your fire. God is not

done with you. You have not seen your
best days. You have to shake off the
blahs. Shake off the discouragement.
There is a flame that is still alive inside
you. The Scripture talks about how we

> *God is not done with you.*
> *You have not seen your*
> *best days.*

must fan the flame, stir up the gifts. It's not enough to just finish.
You have to finish your course with your fire still burning.

Finish Your Course with Joy

For as long as I can remember, my father struggled with high blood
pressure. Toward the end of his life, he didn't feel well. The medi-
cines made him dizzy. His kidneys quit working properly, and he
had to go on dialysis. We used to travel overseas a couple of times a
year. He really looked forward to it. But when his health went downhill, he had to stay at home and take dialysis three times a week. He
never wanted to live if he couldn't preach. Even though he didn't feel
well, he never missed a Sunday.

Victoria used to go pick him up and bring him to church a little
bit late. Sometimes she would call and say, "Joel, I'm not sure your
dad can minister today. It doesn't seem as though he feels well."

I would run down from the TV department during the service.
When he arrived, I would ask, "Daddy, are you sure you're up to this?"

He would smile and say, "Yeah, Joel. I'm ready to go."

When he walked out on the platform, nobody knew he wasn't up to
par. He still had a spring in his step, a smile on his face. He could have
been at home, negative and complaining, "God, I've served You all
these years. Look what it comes down to. I can hardly even minister."

Instead, he kept his fire burning. He guarded that flame. He was
determined to not just finish his course, but to finish it with joy.

One night when my dad was seventy-seven years old, he wasn't feeling well. He asked my brother-in-law Gary to come over and visit with him. They were talking at about two o'clock in the morning and Gary asked him what he thought about the difficulties he was having.

My father said, "Gary, I don't understand it all, but I know this: His mercy endures forever."

Those were the last words my father ever spoke. Right then, he breathed his final breath and went to be with the Lord. But think about those last words. He wasn't complaining. He was bragging on God's goodness. He was not magnifying his problem, but magnifying his God. He crossed the finish line with his fire still burning, with his torch still lit.

> *He crossed the finish line with his fire still burning, with his torch still lit.*

The Scripture talks about how the saints of old died in faith. The truth is that one day we're all going to die. You have to make a decision. Are you going to die in faith? Or are you going to die negative, bitter, and complaining, "I can't believe this happened."

Make up your mind that you're going to die full of joy, with your fire still burning, with your torch still lit.

Never Give Up

In 1968, the Olympic Games were held in Mexico City. During the marathon, a young runner from Tanzania fell and broke his leg. He was bloodied and bruised, but somehow he managed to get up and continue running. Long after everyone else had finished the race, he entered the stadium for his final lap. More than one hundred thousand people had been there earlier, but now, an hour or two later, only a few thousand people remained. The main lights were off, the television cameras gone. The event was officially over.

As he struggled into the stadium and headed toward that final lap, when the few thousand people saw him, they stood up and began to cheer him on. They cheered louder and louder as if he were in first place. Drawing strength from the crowd, he began to smile and wave as if he were going to win the gold medal. It was a moving moment, later seen around the world.

A reporter asked him afterward, "Why didn't you drop out of the race when you broke your leg? Nobody would have faulted you for it." The young man from Tanzania said, "My country didn't send me seven thousand miles to start the race but to finish it."

In the same way, God didn't breathe His life into you, crown you with favor, and put seeds of greatness inside you to just start the race. He sent you to finish it. The Scripture talks about how the race is not for the swift or for the strong, but for those who endure till the end. You don't have to finish first. You're not competing with anybody else. Just finish your course. Keep your fire burning. You weren't created to give up, to quit. We can all find a reason to drop out of the race. We can all find an excuse. But you have to dig your heels in and say, "I am determined to finish my course."

If you will tap into this finishing grace, those two extra cylinders will kick in when you need it. You'll have a strength that you didn't have. As did the Apostle Paul, you will finish your course with joy. You will complete your assignment and become everything God created you to be.

> *Those two extra cylinders will kick in when you need it.*

I AM
STRONG

CHAPTER FOURTEEN

You Can Handle It

We all go through challenges, disappointments, and unfair situations. It's easy to let it overwhelm us to the point where we think, *This is too much. I can't deal with this illness. I can't handle this difficult child.* Or, *I can't take this traffic. It's driving me crazy. This relationship issue, it's going to be the end of me.*

God would not have allowed it if you couldn't handle it. But as long as you're telling yourself it's too much, you'll talk yourself out of it. Have a new perspective. You are not weak. You are full of "can do" power. You are strong in the Lord. All through the day, whether you're stuck in traffic or facing a major disappointment, your attitude should be *I can handle it. I can handle this grouchy boss. I can handle this difficult child. I can handle these people talking about me. I can handle this legal situation.* You can't have a weak, defeated mentality. You have to have a warrior mentality.

> *You can't have a weak, defeated mentality. You have to have a warrior mentality.*

This is what Joseph did. He was betrayed by his brothers, thrown into a pit, sold into slavery, and spent years in a foreign prison for something that he didn't do. But he didn't get depressed. He didn't start complaining. His attitude was, *I can handle it. God is still on the throne. He wouldn't have allowed it unless He had a purpose for it, so I'm going to stay in faith and keep being my best.* In the end, he was made second in charge over all of Egypt. No person, no bad break, no disappointment, and no sickness can keep you from your destiny.

My mother was diagnosed with terminal liver cancer in 1981 and given just a few weeks to live. She could have fallen apart and said, "God, it's not fair. I've served You all these years. I don't understand it." Instead her attitude was, *I can handle it. I'm not a victim. I'm a victor. Nothing can snatch me out of God's hands.* Today, thirty-four years later, my mother is still going strong, healthy, full of joy, full of peace, and helping others.

My father, back in the 1950s, was the pastor of a large denominational church. His future looked very bright. They had just built a beautiful new sanctuary. But through a series of events, my dad had to leave that church. It was a major setback, a big disappointment. He had given years of his life there. But he didn't sit around nursing his wounds. His attitude was, *I can handle it. I know when one door closes, God always opens up another door.* He and my mother went out and launched Lakewood Church, and here we are today still going strong.

"Take Hold of His Strength"

The Apostle Paul put it this way: "I have strength for all things through Christ who empowers me" (Philippians 4:13). Listen to his declaration: "I am ready for anything. I am equal to anything through Him who infuses strength into me." He was saying, "The enemy may hit me with his best shot, but it won't stop me. I'm more than a conqueror."

Paul knew what he was talking about. He had been shipwrecked, spent the night on an open sea, and gone days without food. He was falsely accused, beaten with rods, and thrown into prison. If anyone had a right, at least in the natural, to be negative, bitter, and full of complaint, it would have been Paul. But he understood this principle. His attitude was: *I can handle it. I am ready for and equal to it. Why? Because Almighty God, the Creator of the universe, has infused me with strength. He has equipped me, empowered me, anointed me, crowned me with favor, put royal blood in my veins, and called me to reign in life as a king.*

In difficult times, as Paul did, you have to talk to yourself the right way. If you don't talk to yourself, your thoughts will talk to you. They will tell you, "It's too much. It's never going to change. It's not fair. If God loved you, He would have never let this happen."

The Scripture says, "The rain falls on the just and the unjust." Just because we're a person of faith doesn't exempt us from difficulties. Jesus told a parable about this where one person built their house on a rock. They honored God. Another person built their house on the sand. They didn't honor God. What's interesting is that the same storm came to both people. The wind blew and the rain fell on both houses. The difference is that when you honor God, the storm may come, but when it's all said and done, you will still be standing. The other house built on the sand was washed away. The enemy may hit you with his best shot, but because your house is built on the rock, his best will never be enough. When the storm is over, you will not only come through it, but you'll come out stronger, increased, promoted, and better than you were before.

Now, you have to do what Paul did. Shake off a victim mentality and have a victor mentality. You're not a weakling. You're not lacking. The most powerful

> *"I am ready for and equal to anything that comes my way."*

force in the universe is breathing in your direction. Every morning you need to remind yourself, "I am ready for and equal to anything that comes my way. I am full of 'can do' power. I am strong."

That sickness is no match for you. That relationship issue is not going to keep you from your destiny. The loss of that loved one did not stop God's plan for your life. Don't let it overwhelm you. You can handle it. You've been armed with strength. When you have this warrior mentality, this attitude of faith, knowing that you've been equipped and empowered, all the forces of darkness cannot stop you.

The prophet Isaiah said, "Take hold of His strength." When you make this declaration, "I can handle it," you're not just being positive. You're taking hold of strength. When you say it, you're getting stronger. That's why the Scripture says, "Let the weak *say*, 'I am strong.'" Listen to what you're saying to yourself. "I can't stand this job." "This professor is so difficult. I'll never pass his course." "My loved one didn't make it. I don't know what I'm going to do." If you're always talking about the problem, it's going to drain you. When you talk defeat, strength is leaving. Energy is leaving. Creativity is leaving. Quit letting those things overwhelm you. You are not a victim. You are a victor. If it came your way, you can handle it. You are ready for it and equal to it. If you will stay in agreement with God, He will take what is meant for your harm, and He will use it to your advantage. That difficulty won't defeat you. It will promote you.

Walk Through the Fiery Test

I read about a businessman who had worked for a large home improvement company for more than thirty years. They had retail stores all over the country. He helped build that business from the ground up. But one day they had a corporate restructuring. They decided that they no longer needed him. Of course, he was disappointed. It didn't seem fair. But instead of sitting around nursing his wounds, thinking about what he lost, he had the attitude, *I can handle it. This is not going to defeat me. It's going to promote me.*

In difficult times you have to remind yourself that nothing is a surprise to God. He's not up in the heavens scratching His head, saying, "Oh, man, he got laid off. That messed everything up." "Oh, she was diagnosed with cancer." "Joseph got thrown into a pit. Now what am I going to do?" God knows the end from the beginning. He has already written every day of your life in His book. The good news is, if you will stay in faith, your book ends in victory.

This executive, instead of looking for another job, got a couple of his friends together, and they started their own company. They called it "The Home Depot." It's become one of the largest, most successful home improvement stores in the world. What am I saying? That difficulty is not meant to defeat you. It's meant to promote you. A setback is simply a setup for a greater comeback.

"Well, Joel. It's so hard, and I don't understand it. It doesn't seem fair."

You're talking yourself into defeat. If it came your way, you can handle it. Start talking to yourself in a new way. "I am well able. I am equipped. I am empowered. I am ready for anything."

The fact is that God is not going to deliver us from every difficulty. He is not going to keep us from every challenge. If He did, we would never grow. The Scripture says, "Our faith is tried in the fire of affliction." When you're in a tough time, that's an opportunity to show God what you're made of. Anybody can get negative and bitter and blame God. It's easy to lose your passion. But if you want to pass the test, if you want God to take you to a new level, you can't be a weakling. You have to be a warrior. Dig your heels in and declare with Paul, "I can handle it. I'm ready for it. I'm equal to it. I know

God is still on the throne. He is fighting my battles, and on the other side of this difficulty is a new level of my destiny."

Colossians 3:12 says, "God has given us the power to endure whatever comes our way with a good attitude." Maybe at the office you're not being treated fairly. It's one thing to go to work negative, discouraged, complaining, and bad-mouthing the boss. That doesn't take any faith. But if you want to pass the test, you have to go to work with a smile on your face, with a positive attitude, being good to people, doing more than you're required. At your home, maybe your spouse or your kids are not treating you the way they should. It's easy to think, *I'm going to treat him the way he is treating me.* Or, *These kids are disrespectful. I'm not going to give them the time of day.* But if you want to pass the test, you have to be good to people even when they're not being good to you. You have to do the right thing when the wrong thing is happening. See it as an opportunity to grow. Every time you do the right thing, a blessing will follow. When you take the high road, there will always be a reward.

> If you want to pass the test, you have to be good to people even when they're not being good to you.

Too often the mistake we make is to constantly tell ourselves, "It's not fair. It's not right. When they change, when it improves, then I'll have a better attitude." You have to make the first move. You do your part, and God will do His part. Quit worrying about God changing another person, and first allow God to change you. Is there something you're letting overwhelm you? You think it's too much. Why don't you get up every morning and make this declaration: "God, I want to thank You that I can handle anything that comes my way today. I can handle a difficult boss. I can handle getting stuck in traffic. I can handle my plans not working out. Lord, thank You that I'll have a good attitude wherever I am." You have to decide before you leave the house that nothing that comes your way is going to upset you. Decide ahead of time.

All Things Will Work Out for Your Good

A friend of mine was going to have her family over for dinner on Christmas Eve, and then they were going to her in-laws for a Christmas Day lunch. She was in charge of bringing desserts for both parties. She is a very organized, detailed person. A couple of weeks before Christmas, she called her favorite bakery, where she had ordered desserts many times before. This time she ordered seven pies: two pecan, two pumpkin, two chess, and one lemon meringue pie. She had to work on the morning of Christmas Eve, and in the afternoon she was going to drive with her mother to the bakery and pick up the pies. But that day a snowstorm unexpectedly came in. The roads were very difficult to travel. The whole city was frozen over. Nevertheless, she and her mom braved the bad weather. They finally made it to the bakery just before it closed on Christmas Eve.

My friend walked up to the counter, handed the young man her receipt, and said, "I'm here to pick up my seven pies."

He shook his head and said, "I'm sorry, ma'am. We don't have any more pies."

She said, "That's impossible. I ordered these two weeks ago. I have to have these pies for my Christmas dinners."

He repeated, "I'm sorry. The weather was so bad that we didn't think anybody else would come in, so we've sold all the pies."

She was very upset. She started telling her mother how wrong that was and how she was going to call the owner, how it was ruining her Christmas, on and on.

Another customer had come in behind them and overheard everything that was going on. This lady walked up to my friend with a big smile and said, "Hey, it's Christmas. Why are you so upset? I'm going to pray that you find your desserts."

My friend rolled her eyes and thought, *Lady, I don't need prayer. I need pies.* She thanked the lady for praying, then she and her mother exited the bakery and got back in the car.

Her mother said, "Why don't we call the other bakery across town?"

Exasperated, my friend replied, "Oh, Mom, we'll never get across town in this bad weather. Plus, they're not going to have any pies left late on Christmas Eve." Her mother finally talked her into calling the bakery. When she asked if they had any pies, the lady said, "Let me check." She came back on the line and said, "All we have left are seven pies: two pecan, two pumpkin, two chess, and one lemon meringue."

Friend, God is in complete control. You don't have to get upset when things don't go your way. You have the power to remain calm. You can handle any situation. Quit letting little things steal your joy. Every day is a gift from God. Life is too short to live it negative, offended, bitter, and discouraged. Start passing the tests.

> *You have the power to remain calm. You can handle any situation.*

Start believing that God is directing your steps. Believe that He is in control of your life. Believe that He has solutions to problems that you haven't even had. If you will stay calm and stay in faith, God promises that all things will work out for your good.

"Well, Joel," you say, "I was in that same type of situation, but it didn't have a good end. They didn't have any pies left." Maybe God is trying to help you lose some weight. You can handle it!

Things Will Not Stick to You

We've all seen how a spider spins a web in order to catch an insect. That web is filled with a sticky substance, so when an insect comes in contact with it, it not only gets tangled in the web, but it actually gets stuck. Have you ever wondered how the spider that's spinning the sticky web can walk across it and not get stuck? It seems as though it would get trapped in its own web. But God made the spider so that its body releases a special oil that flows down to the legs. That way it can just slide across the web. You could say the spider doesn't get stuck because of the anointing that's on its life. In a similar way, God has put an anointing on your life. It's like oil that causes things not to stick.

When you walk in your anointing, knowing that you can handle anything that comes your way, things that should bring you down won't be able to. You get laid off. It wasn't fair. You should be discouraged. You should be upset, but you stay in faith and you end up with a better job. A relationship comes to an end. You should be bitter, should be discouraged, but you keep moving forward, and God opens up a new door. At the office, people are playing politics, talking behind your back. You might try to get even. You might try to pay them back, but because of this anointing, it just slides right off you.

Perhaps you wonder, as I did, *How did I make it through the loss of my father?* How did you make it through that slow season at work? How did you make it through that illness, that breakup? It's because of the anointing God put on your life. He gave you strength when you didn't think you could go on. He gave you joy when you should have been discouraged. He made a way when it looked impossible. Now we can all say with David, "Where would we be without the goodness of God?" Bottom line: God has infused strength into you. He has equipped and empowered you. You are ready for and equal to anything that comes your way. When you face difficulties, remind yourself, "I am anointed for this. I'm not going to fall apart. I'm not going to start complaining. I can handle it. I know God is still on the throne. He is fighting my battles, and if God be for me, who dare be against me?"

Another friend of mine has had cancer three times. I've never once heard him complain. I've never seen him depressed. We used to play basketball together. Nobody even knew anything was wrong. He doesn't have a weak, defeated "poor old me" mentality. He's got a warrior mentality. He knows he can handle it. He's anointed for it. A couple of years ago, the cancer came back for the third time. The doctors told him that before he took chemo they were going to harvest his white blood cells, which they could use to help restore his immune system after the treatment. He asked the doctors how many of these cells they needed. They gave him a number. He said, "Doctors, I'm going to give you twice what you need."

For the next couple of months, all through the day he would go around saying, "Father, thank You that my white blood cells are multiplying. They're getting stronger, increasing. They will do exactly what You have created them to do." What was he doing? Talking to himself. Taking hold of that strength.

He went back to the doctors, who said, "You're a man of your word. You've given us four times the amount that we were hoping for." He took that treatment, and today he is totally cancer free, healthy, and strong.

Refuse to Give Up

The Scripture says in Philippians 1:28, "Do not be intimidated by your enemies." Don't be intimidated by that cancer. It's no match for you. Sickness cannot keep you from your destiny. God has you in the

palm of His hand. Nothing can snatch you away. If it's not your time
to go, you're not going to go. Don't be
intimidated by that financial problem.   *"Do not be intimidated."*
Don't be intimidated by what some-
body said about you. There is an anointing on your life that seals you,
protects you, enables you, and empowers you. God has infused you
with strength. The Scripture calls it "can do" power.

I was at the beach one time when our children were much smaller.
Alexandra was three years old, and Jonathan was six. We were having a good time, playing in the sand, making castles, when this little yellow bumblebee came and landed right beside Alexandra. She
took off running, afraid. I swatted the bee out of the way. We went
back to playing. About thirty seconds later, that bumblebee was
right back flying all around. My kids started screaming, "Daddy!
Get him! Get him!" I grabbed my towel, and knocked him down to
the sand. I thought, *I showed him who's the boss!*

About a minute later, there the bumblebee was again, buzzing all
around, flying by our heads. This time I grabbed my towel and not
only knocked him down to the sand, but I got my tennis shoe and
squashed him into the sand as hard as I possibly could. I was tired
of dealing with him. We went back to playing. A couple of minutes
later, I looked over just to make sure he was still dead. I couldn't
believe it. I noticed one wing start to move. Then the other wing
came up out of the sand. I thought, *This is the bumblebee from hell.*
He started walking across the sand as though he was dazed. I was
amazed that not only was he alive, but that he could get back up
again. About that time, he started flying off away from me.

Just when I thought he had learned his lesson—"Don't mess with
Joel"—that bumblebee turned around and came right back and buzzed
by my head at least three or four times. I had to dodge to get out of the
way. It was just like he was saying, "Ha-ha-ha! You couldn't kill me."

Alexandra exclaimed, "Daddy, kill him for good this time!"

I replied, "No, Alexandra. This bumblebee deserves to live. I'm a thousand times bigger than him, and I still couldn't keep him down."

That's the way you need to see yourself. No matter how big that enemy looks. No matter how powerful it may seem. There is a force in you that is more powerful than any opposition. Greater is He that is in you than anything that comes against you. Just be like that bumblebee—refuse to give up, refuse to fall into self-pity, refuse to be overwhelmed. Instead, have this attitude: *I'm ready for and equal to anything that comes my way. I've been anointed with "can do" power. I am armed with strength for this battle.* When you have this warrior mentality, this "I can handle it" attitude, all the forces of darkness cannot keep you from your destiny.

Perhaps you've already decided, *I can't handle this sickness anymore. I can't handle this problem at work. I can't handle taking care of my elderly parents and my family, too.* Quit telling yourself it's too much. Those negative, defeated thoughts are draining your energy. You wouldn't be there if you couldn't handle it. God would not have allowed it if you weren't ready for it and equal to it. You're anointed for it. When you press past what's coming against you, on the other side of that difficulty is a new level of your destiny.

> *When you press past what's coming against you, on the other side of that difficulty is a new level of your destiny.*

You Will Come Out Better

I heard about a wealthy man who was known for being very eccentric, far out. One night he was having a big party at his house. In his backyard, his swimming pool was filled with sharks and alligators.

He announced to all the guests, "Anyone who will swim across my pool, I will give you anything that you want."

In a few minutes there was a big splash. He looked over, and this man was swimming ninety to nothing, dodging the alligators, maneuvering his way around the sharks, as frantic as could be. He made it to the other side just in the nick of time and jumped out totally panicked.

The wealthy man came over and said, "I can't believe it. You're the bravest person I've ever met. Now, what do you want me to give you?"

The man looked around the pool and answered, "What I want more than anything else is the name of the person who just pushed me in!"

Here's my point: Sometimes in life it feels as though we got pushed in. We weren't expecting it. A bad medical report. The relationship didn't make it. A business goes down. It may be a surprise to us, but it is not a surprise to God. If you get pushed in, don't sit around nursing your wounds. Do as this man did and just go for it. Just keep being your best. Keep honoring God. Keep doing what you know you're supposed to do. God has already given you the strength, the wisdom, the favor, and the determination not only to make it through, but to come out better than you were before.

Remember, that difficulty is not going to defeat you. It's going to promote you. You can handle it. Take hold of this strength. Get up every morning and remind yourself, "I'm ready for and equal to anything that comes my way. I am strong." If you will do this, God promises He will infuse strength into you. You will overcome every obstacle, defeat every enemy, and live the victorious life that belongs to you.

I AM
ANOINTED

CHAPTER FIFTEEN

You Are Anointed

We don't have to go through life doing everything on our own, trying to accomplish our dreams only in our own ability, trying to overcome challenges in our own strength, our own intellect, and our own hard work. We have an advantage. God has placed His anointing on you. The anointing is a divine empowerment. It enables you to do what you could not do on your own. It will cause you to accomplish dreams even though you don't have the talent. It will help you overcome obstacles that looked insurmountable.

I've heard it said, "The anointing to us is like gasoline to a car." You can have the most expensive car with a huge engine, a beautiful exterior, and luxuries inside, but if you don't put gasoline in it, it's not going to do you much good. In a similar way, you've been made in the image of Almighty God. You are full of incredible potential. You have seeds of greatness. The fuel you need to release your greatness, to overcome obstacles, and to accomplish dreams is the anointing on your life. The anointing is only activated where there is faith. Instead of complaining about how it's not going to work out or how

> "The anointing to us is like gasoline to a car."

you'll never accomplish your dreams, turn that around and start declaring, "I am anointed. I am equipped. I am empowered. I am well able." When you have this attitude of faith and are speaking words of victory, you are putting fuel in your car. You're stirring up your anointing. That's when you'll go places that you couldn't go on your own. That's when you'll see breakthroughs. Situations will suddenly change in your favor.

You may work around people who are negative and hard to get along with. It's easy to think, *I can't stand going to work. These people get on my nerves.* That's draining your fuel. Your car is not going to run properly. God wouldn't have you there if you couldn't handle it. Have a new perspective. You've been anointed to work in that difficult environment. You're anointed to put up with cranky coworkers. You're anointed to deal with a grouchy boss. Quit telling yourself how difficult it is and start declaring, "I am anointed. I'm going to enjoy my job. I'm going to put a smile on my face. I'm going to be good to people. This is the day the Lord has made. I'm going to choose to be happy." When you do that, God will fight your battles. God will move the wrong people out of the way. He will get you to where you're supposed to be.

Maybe you're raising a child who's difficult. It's taking a lot of time and effort. You don't see how you can keep doing it. You have to remind yourself that you are anointed to raise your child. God didn't just put you there and say, "All right. Good luck. You're on your own. Let's see what you can do." He has already equipped and empowered you for every situation. Stop talking about how hard it is and start declaring, "I can do all things through Christ. I am strong in the Lord. I am well able to raise my children." You have to stir up the anointing. That's what keeps you moving forward.

Perhaps you're dealing with an illness. It hit you unexpectedly. You could be discouraged, let it overwhelm you, and complain, "I can't believe this is happening to me." Instead, have a new perspective. That sickness is not a surprise to God. It didn't catch God off guard. He has already anointed you. You have the strength, the peace, the determination, and the confidence you need. You're not lacking. You're anointed. The forces that are for you are greater than the forces that are against you. In those difficult times, you have to declare what Isaiah stated: "The anointing on my life is breaking every yoke." "The anointing is greater than this cancer." "The anointing is greater than this depression." "The anointing is causing me to overcome." Every time you say, "I am anointed," chains are broken. Fear has to leave. Depression has to go. Healing comes. Strength comes. Faith comes.

Your Time Is Coming

When David was a teenager, the prophet Samuel came to his house and anointed him to be the next king of Israel. Out of all of Jesse's sons, Samuel picked out David and poured the anointing oil on his head. What's interesting is that after Samuel anointed him, he sent David back to the shepherd's fields to take care of the sheep. David lived as a shepherd for years even though he had a king's anointing. The Scripture tells us to "reign in life as a king." Every one of you has a king's anointing, a queen's anointing. This means to live an abundant life, to accomplish your God-given dreams, to raise children who will be mighty in the land, to leave your mark on this generation.

But as was true for David, even though you've been anointed, on the way to your destiny there will be times of testing, where you don't see anything happening, times of waiting when you have to be patient and keep doing the right things, times when it doesn't look as though it's ever going to change. You have to stay in faith and keep believing, *My time is coming. God has spoken it over me. He has put the promise in my heart. I may not see how it can happen. The odds may be against me. But I have a secret weapon. The anointing is on my life.*

If you will stay in faith and don't get discouraged or talk yourself out of it because it's not happening on your timetable, God will get you to where you're supposed to be. God knows what He is doing. He hasn't forgotten about you. You may think you don't have the skill, the talent, or the experience to accomplish what's in your heart, but that's okay. The anointing on your life will make up for what you don't have. You can have less talent, but with the anointing you will go further than people who have more talent. It is not just your intellect, your expertise, or your experience that determines how high you're going to go. It's the fact that Almighty God is breathing on your life. The anointing will cause you to accomplish dreams you could never accomplish on your own. It will propel you into your destiny.

> *The anointing on your life will make up for what you don't have.*

You're Not "Just" Anything

This is what happened to a woman in the Scripture named Deborah. In the book of Judges she describes herself as "a mother in Israel." This was significant. It was saying she wasn't working in the corporate world. She didn't have an impressive position, title, influence, or prestige. She wasn't necessarily super talented or highly educated. She was a mother raising her children. Back in those days, women didn't have the leadership roles that they have today. They were seen as secondary, with no influence. Deborah would have been considered "just a mother."

But can I tell you, you're not "just" anything! You're a child of the Most High God. People may try to dismiss you, discount you, and push you down. "You don't have the talent, the training, the position, or the title. You come from the wrong family." What they can't see is that God has put something on you that supersedes all of that, something that causes you to break barriers, to excel, to accomplish dreams, to do what you could not do. I'm all for getting the best education you can, for developing your talents and improving your skills, but you are not limited to your own ability, your own education, your own intellect, or your own experience. Those will take you to a certain level, but to reach your highest potential you need the anointing on your life. You need God to open doors that you can't open. You need favor that you don't have to work for, good

> *You are not limited to your own ability, your own education, your own intellect, or your own experience.*

breaks that you don't deserve, and wisdom that you don't learn in school. That's what the anointing does. It takes you where you could not go on your own.

This mother in Israel, Deborah, was living in a nation that was overcome with violence and all kinds of mayhem. The main roads had gotten so bad they couldn't even be traveled. People were constantly being attacked and robbed; there was no order. It looked as if that's the way it would always be. But God put a dream in Deborah's heart to do something about it. She could have come up with plenty of excuses. "God, I'm just a woman. Nobody is going to listen to me. I'm just a mother raising my child. I'm not in the government. I don't have anybody backing me up—no police force, no army." But

Deborah understood this principle. She knew God had put something on her that would cause her to excel.

The Scripture says that the highways were unoccupied and that Israel had been held in bondage for twenty years until Deborah, a mother in Israel, arose. Deborah took a step of faith, and other people began to join in. Before long the enemy's army was destroyed and order was restored. Everything had turned around. The nation was calm and peaceful.

How could this mother affect the whole nation? It was the anointing on her life. You are not limited by who you know, by how influential you are, or by how much income you have. There is something that supersedes talent, income, and experience. It's the anointing God has placed on your life. Quit making excuses as to what you can't do. "Joel, I'm just a mom." A mom with the anointing is more powerful than a CEO without it! "Well, I'm just a student." "I'm just a businessperson." "I'm just an accountant. I can't do anything great." Why not? Deborah, a mother, changed her whole nation. I can tell you firsthand, I'm not the most talented person. I don't have the most experience, the most training, or the most education, but I do have the anointing. So do you.

In Due Season You Will Reap

When my father went to be with the Lord back in 1999, I stepped up to pastor the church although I had never ministered before. Every voice told me, "You are not a minister. You can't get up there in front of people. You're not going to know what to say. Nobody is going to listen to you." Instead of dwelling on those thoughts, I would look at myself in the mirror and say, "Joel, you are anointed. You're the man for the job. This is your moment. You've been raised up for such a time as this." What was I doing? Adding fuel to my car. I was stirring up the anointing.

There will always be negative voices that try to talk you out of your dreams, try to convince you to settle where you are, but let me encourage you. You're the man or woman for the job. You've been raised up. You have what it takes. You're qualified. You're anointed. You're approved. You're talented enough. You're strong enough. You're experienced enough. You and God are a majority. Quit discounting yourself. Quit making excuses.

If you will start taking steps of faith, doing what you can, God will do what you can't. He will bring the right people and open the right doors. He will give you the wisdom and the creativity. He will make it all come together. Don't settle for mediocrity. You were created for greatness. You have a king's anointing. You may be in the shepherd's fields right now. It may feel as though you're doing something insignificant, but where you are is not where you're staying. That's not permanent. That's temporary. You are going to come out.

> *You were created for greatness. You have a king's anointing.*

You haven't reached your highest potential. Start talking to yourself the right way. "I'm the right person for the job. This is my moment. I've been raised up. I'm going to step into the fullness of my destiny."

David spent years in the shepherd's fields, but the key was he never forgot he had a king's anointing. It would have been easy for him to think, *I must have heard Samuel wrong. I know he anointed me, but I sure haven't become the king. He must have missed it this time.* No, every day he kept reminding himself, "I am anointed. My time is coming. I will make a difference with my life." What was he doing? Adding fuel to his car. It didn't look as though he was going anywhere. It sounded as though he was just wasting his breath and getting his hopes up, but God sees what you're doing and hears what you're saying. Every day that you live in faith, with expectancy, you are one day closer to seeing your dreams come to pass. God knows when the right time is. If it hasn't happened yet, that means it's still on the way. God is getting you prepared. You're growing. You're getting stronger. Sometimes God knows the blessing is going to be so big we couldn't handle it if it happened right now, so He is getting us matured. What God has in your future is going to be greater than anything you've seen in the past.

Paul said it this way: "Don't get tired of doing what's right. In due season you will reap, if you don't give up." Your due season is coming. You're going to step into that king's anointing, that queen's anointing. You're just getting started. God's dream for your life is so much bigger than your own. If He would have done it earlier, you wouldn't have been prepared. Now is your time. You're about to step into what you were created to do. You're going to step into a new level of your destiny. The disappointments, the delays, and the setbacks in the past were all a part of the plan to get you prepared for right now. Nothing was wasted. It strengthened you. You developed trust, endurance, and confidence. Now you're prepared for this time. You're on the runway about to take off. You're going to see the exceeding greatness of God's favor!

Your Cup Will Run Over

David was out in the shepherd's fields. It didn't look like anything was happening, but he came into his due season. King Saul sent a message saying, "Send me David who is with the sheep. I need him in the palace." David started working for Saul. That was another step on the way to his destiny. He wasn't on the throne yet, but at least he made it to the palace. Notice this phrase: "Send David, who is with the sheep…" You may feel like you're with the sheep today. In other words, you're doing something that feels insignificant. You know you have more in you, but you've been in the background year after year. Don't get discouraged. Your time is coming. You're not going to stay with the sheep. God is going to take you from the background to the foreground. You may be in the shepherd's fields, but don't put your stakes down. Don't get comfortable there. You have a king's anointing. You are destined to do great

> *You may be in the shepherd's fields, but don't get comfortable there.*

things. The palace is coming. Victory is coming. Promotion is coming. People can't stop it. Bad breaks can't stop it. Sickness can't stop it. Almighty God has anointed you. What He has spoken over your life will come to pass.

I talked to a single mother a few years ago. She told me about how it was such a struggle to make ends meet. She was having to work two jobs, long hours. She felt bad that she couldn't be there with her children. She had no free time to date or have any kind of social life. It looked as though it would always be that way. She was "with the sheep," so to speak. She was in the shepherd's fields. She could have gotten discouraged and settled there, but she knew deep down she had this queen's anointing. She knew she was made for more than just constantly struggling, enduring, and not having enough. She kept reminding herself that the anointing can break any yoke. Poverty, lack, and barely getting by are a yoke. Do not accept that as your destiny. Jesus came that you might live an abundant life. We are to be the head and not the tail. And yes, we all go through dry seasons, but they are not permanent. They are temporary. At some point the drought will come to an end, and you will see an abundance of rain, an abundance of favor.

I like how David put it in Psalm 23. He said, "God anoints my head with oil." He went on to say, "Because I am anointed, my cup runs over." When you walk in your anointing, knowing who you are and whose you are, at some point your cup will run over. You will see God pour out blessings that you cannot contain. Don't you dare settle with the sheep in the shepherd's fields. The palace is coming.

One day the single mother was invited to dinner by a couple that lived down the street from her whom she had only met once. That night they handed her the keys to a brand-new car that they had bought for her. She was able to sell her car and pay off most of her debts so she didn't have to work so much. Just recently I learned she married an executive from a large company. Now she and her children are no longer with the sheep. They're in the palace. God has blessed them. He has done exceedingly, abundantly above and beyond.

Friend, you were not created to barely get by, to take the leftovers, to live out in the shepherd's fields. You were created for victory, for abundance, for the palace. The same God who increased the single mother can increase you. The anointing on your life will cause people to be good to you. It will cause you to be at the right place at the right time, bringing favor, promotion, and increase.

Fresh Anointings

David was in the palace playing the harp for King Saul. It was a temporary position. He wasn't supposed to be there long. But David was so good at what he did, King Saul created a new position exclusively for David. He became an armor bearer. If you will be your best right where you are and excel in what you do, the right doors will always open for you. There may not be room for promotion at your work as far as you can see right now, but don't worry. Your gifts will make room for you. If there is not a position, God can cause them to create a new position. Maybe you are part-time, believing for more work. You need to get ready. As David did, you're going to become full-time. You've passed the test. You've been faithful in the shepherd's fields. You knew you had more in you and you didn't slack off. You didn't complain. You stayed in faith, trusting God's timing. Now your due season has come. You're going to step into that king's anointing. What God promised you, He will bring to pass.

Years later, King Saul was killed in a battle. Now it was David's time. He was thirty years old and about to take the throne. At this time, Israel was divided into two kingdoms—Judah and Israel. Second Samuel 2 says, "The men of Judah came and anointed David king over Judah." He served there seven and a half years, then he brought the two kingdoms together. When he was thirty-seven years old, the men of Israel joined the men of Judah, and they anointed David again to be the king over all of Israel.

What's interesting is that David was anointed as a teenager to become the king. When the men of Judah came to anoint him again, he could have said, "Guys, I've already been anointed. No need. It happened when I was a teenager. Samuel did it." Seven and a half years later when the men of Israel came to anoint him king over all of Israel, he could have said, "This is not necessary. I was anointed twice already. I don't need to be anointed again." But David understood the importance of

> *You can't win today's battles on yesterday's anointing. You need to have a fresh anointing.*

having a fresh anointing. You can't win today's battles on yesterday's anointing. You need to have a fresh anointing.

Too often we are trying to do things in our own strength. It's a struggle. No promotion. No increase. It's weighing us down. We don't realize that all we have to say is, "God, I need a fresh anointing.

God, fill me with new strength, new ideas, new creativity, and new passion." When you do that, God will breathe freshness onto your life. The reason things get stale and we just endure our marriage, endure the job, and drag through the day is we're not stirring up the anointing. On a regular basis we need to pray, "God, I need a fresh anointing in my marriage, a fresh anointing on my career, a fresh anointing on my mind and my thoughts. God, help me to see things from the right perspective."

The Anointing Breaks the Yoke

If David would have taken the throne without the fresh anointing, he wouldn't have had the success and the favor that he had. When you humble yourself and say, "God, I can't do this on my own. I need Your help. I need Your favor. I need Your wisdom. God, I need a fresh anointing," you're showing your dependency on Him. When you acknowledge God in that way, He will give you wisdom beyond your years. He will help you accomplish things that you could have never accomplished on your own. Whenever you start a new job or even a new position, always ask for that fresh anointing. Parents, when you have a baby, pray, "God, give me a fresh anointing to raise this child." Students, when you start a new class, humbly ask, "God, give me a fresh anointing for this semester." You're saying, "God, I'm ready for new opportunities, new abilities, new friendships, and new ideas." Maybe you're facing a challenge today—your health, your finances, a relationship. Instead of complaining about it, why don't you say, "God, give me a fresh anointing to overcome this challenge." It's the anointing that breaks the yoke.

Just as the men of Judah anointed David for his new season, I believe today God is releasing a fresh anointing in your life. You're going to go where you've never been. You're going to see negative situations turn around. Chains of addictions and bad habits are being broken. Healing, promotion, and restoration are coming. You're going to step into the fullness of your destiny. Friend, you have a king's anointing, a queen's anointing. Don't settle for mediocrity. Stir up the

> *You're going to go where you've never been.*

anointing. Every morning remind yourself, "I am anointed. I am equipped. I am empowered." Remember to always ask for that fresh anointing. If you do this, I believe and declare, as David did, you will make it to your throne and step into the fullness of your destiny.

I AM
PATIENT

CHAPTER SIXTEEN

Trust God's Timing

In life we're always waiting for something—waiting for a dream to come to pass, waiting to meet the right person, waiting for a problem to turn around. When it's not happening as fast as we would like, it's easy to get frustrated. But you have to realize that the moment you prayed, God established a set time to bring the promise to pass. God has a set time for you to meet the right person. There is a set time for the problem to turn around, a set time for your healing, your promotion, and your breakthrough. It may be tomorrow, or next week, or five years from now.

But when you understand that the time has already been set, it takes all the pressure off. You won't live worried, wondering when this is ever going to happen. You'll relax and enjoy your life, knowing that the promise has already been scheduled by the Creator of the universe.

Maybe you have been praying about a situation for a long time and don't see anything happening. You could easily be discouraged. But what if God were to pull back the curtain and allow you to see into the future, and you saw that on February 12 at 2:33 in the afternoon, you were going to meet the person of your dreams? You wouldn't be discouraged. You would be excited. You would start working out and go buy some new clothes. Why? You know the big day is coming.

Here's where it takes faith. God promises that there are set times in our future, but He doesn't tell us when they will be. Your set time may be tomorrow morning at 9:47. You'll get the phone call you've been waiting for. Your set time may be October 25, two years from now. You'll get a good break, and that will thrust you to a new level.

> *Your set time may be tomorrow morning at 9:47.*

My question is, "Do you trust God enough to believe that your set times are coming?" Are you willing to wait with a good attitude, knowing that they're on the way? Or will you get discouraged and think, *I don't know, Joel. I've been trying to break this addiction since high school.* You have to have a new perspective. God has a set time for you to break that addiction. It's already in your future. Don't let the negative thoughts talk you out of it. There is a set time for you to be completely well, a set time for God to turn the legal situation around. Now, quit worrying about it. Quit living stressed out, thinking, *What if I don't meet the right person? What if I don't ever get well?*

"Wait Patiently, for It Shall Surely Come"

The Scripture says, "Those who have believed enter into the rest of God." The way you know you're really believing is that you have a rest. You're at peace. You know the answer is on the way. You know the right people and the right opportunities have already been set in your future.

On January 8, 1986, at four o'clock in the afternoon, I walked into a jewelry store to buy a battery for my watch. Out walked the most beautiful girl I had ever seen. It was Victoria. I didn't tell her, but I thought, *This is my set time.* It took me a year to convince her that it was her set time, too!

On December 3, 2003, at one thirty in the afternoon, when Mayor Brown handed us the keys to the Compaq Center, that was not an ordinary time. That was a set time ordained by the Most High God.

In the same way, there are set times in your future. You've prayed, believed, and stood in faith. Let me assure you that you're going to come into set times of favor, a set time where a problem suddenly turns around, a set time where you meet the right person, a set time where a good break thrusts you years ahead.

That's what Habakkuk said. "The vision is for an appointed time. It may seem slow in coming, but wait patiently, for it will surely come." Not "maybe come." Not "I hope so." God has already set the date. The appointed time has already been put on your calendar. One translation says, "It won't be one second late."

> *"The vision is for an appointed time."*

Sometimes we think, *Everybody is getting ahead of me. My friends are all married, and I'm still single. My coworkers are being promoted, but I'm still stuck here.* Don't get discouraged. God knows how to make up for what seems like lost time. God doesn't always take us logically from A to B to C. Sometimes God will take you from A to B to C, and then thrust you all the way down to S, T, U, V. What happened? You hit a set time that pushed you fifty years ahead. Quit worrying about who's getting ahead of you and just run your race. Be the best that you can be. Keep honoring God with your life. Keep treating people right, and God will get you to where you're supposed to be. That promotion, that healing, that breakthrough, and that right person won't be one second late. Our God is not a random God. He is a precise God. He has lined up solutions for you down to the very second.

I know a young lady who was believing to meet the right man. She was in her early thirties and had never really had a serious relationship with anyone. She was starting to wonder if it was going to happen. One day she was driving home from work, had a flat tire, and pulled over on the side of the freeway. In a few seconds, another car pulled over. Out stepped a handsome young man who came up to her window and said, "Can I help you?"

She took one look at him and said, *"I think you can."*

He not only changed her tire, but he invited her out to dinner. They ended up falling in love. A year and a half later, they got married. Today, they're as happy as can be. That wasn't a coincidence. It wasn't a lucky break. That was a set time ordained by the Creator of the universe. Think about how precise God's timing is. The tire had to go flat at just the right time. An hour later, and it wouldn't have happened. There had to be just the right amount of traffic. Too many cars, and he would've been late. Too few cars, and he would've been early. He had to leave his work at just the right time. One extra fifteen-minute phone call and that would have never worked out. The timing was down to the split second for it to all fall into place.

The Appointed Time Is the Best Time

What am I saying? You can trust God's timing. God has it all figured out. What you're praying about and what you're believing for are not going to be one second late. If it hasn't happened yet, it doesn't mean something is wrong. It doesn't mean God is mad at you. It doesn't mean it's never going to work out. God has already established the time down to the split second. You don't have to worry. You don't have to live frustrated. Stay in peace. Enter into this rest. God has you in the palm of His hand. Your steps are being directed by the Creator of the universe; not randomly, not vaguely. Down to the millisecond. Down to the most finite, small detail. When you understand this, it takes all of the pressure off. You won't go around wondering when something is going to happen.

> *When you know the time has been set, you'll have a peace.*

"God, when are You going to change my husband? God, when are You going to answer my prayer?" When you know the time has been set, you'll have a peace. Whether it's twenty minutes or twenty years, you know that what God promised He will bring to pass.

A great prayer we should pray every day is, "God, give me the grace to accept Your timing." I'd love to tell you that if you stay in faith, if you believe, God will always answer your prayer within twenty-four hours, or at least within the first week. But we know that's not reality. God promises He will be true to His Word, but He never puts a time frame on it. It would be a lot easier if God told us when we were going to get well, when we would meet the right person, or when our child would straighten up. But that wouldn't take any faith. It takes faith to say, "God, I don't know *when* You are going to do it, but I trust You enough to believe that You *will* do it, that the answer is already in my future."

The Scripture says, "The vision is for an appointed time." The appointed time is the best time. God can see the big picture for our lives. He knows what's up ahead. He knows what we're going to need, who we're going to need, and when they need to show up. If God did everything we ask on our timetable, it would limit us. Because sometimes, what we're asking for is too small. Gods knows that the person we think we can't live without is not going to be good for us in ten years, so He is closing the door right now. God knows that if He gave us that promotion we want so badly right now, it would keep us from the much bigger promotion He has in store for us three years down the road. God has the advantage of seeing it all. The longer I live, the more I trust Him. How many times have I looked back and said, "God, thank You for not answering that prayer. Thank You for not letting that person into my life." God knows what He is doing.

What you're praying about may be good. It may be a part of your destiny, but it's not the appointed time. If there is a right time, that means there is a wrong time. If it hasn't happened yet, instead of being frustrated and worried and asking, "God, when is my business going to grow? God, I'm so lonely. When am I going to meet somebody?" have a new approach. "God, You know what's best for me. You can see the big picture. I'm not going to live frustrated. God, I trust Your timing."

Don't Expect It to Happen on Your Timetable

We live in a society that wants everything right now. We're being programmed for immediacy. Don't make me wait. But the Scripture says, "It's through faith and patience that we inherit the promises." It's easy to have faith. "God, I believe I'm going to accomplish my dreams. God, I believe I'm going to overcome this obstacle." We have the faith part down. Let's make sure we get the patience part down. "God, I'm not only going to believe for big things, but I trust Your timing. I'm not going to get discouraged if it doesn't happen immediately. I'm not going to give up because it's

> *"It's through faith and patience that we inherit the promises."*

taken a week, a month, or five years. I know the set time is already in my future, so I'm going to wait with faith and patience because I know that it's on the way."

When Victoria was pregnant with our son, Jonathan, the first few months were very exciting. Not a problem at all. But about six months in, Victoria started getting uncomfortable. Her feet started swelling. By the seventh month, her back was hurting. She couldn't sleep well at night. By the eight month, she was saying, "God, I want to have this baby right now. I am tired of waiting." But we knew God had an appointed time. The child was not ready. It was still growing, developing. If God let her have the baby early, the child may not have been healthy.

Sometimes we pray, "God, give me this promise right now. I'm uncomfortable. These people aren't treating me right. Business is slow." What we can't see is that something is not ready. Maybe it's another person who's going to be involved. God is still working on them. Maybe it's another situation that's going to be a part of your destiny. It's not in place yet. Or maybe God is doing a work in you, developing your character, growing you stronger in that process.

The Scripture says, "God didn't take the Israelites the shortest route to the Promised Land, because He knew they were not prepared for war." God could see the big picture. He knew that if He took them the shortest way, their enemies would be too powerful and they would be defeated. So on purpose, God took them a longer route to protect them and to strengthen them so that they could fulfill their destiny.

If something is not happening on your timetable, remind yourself, "God knows what He is doing. He has my best interests at heart. I wouldn't be having this delay unless God had a very good reason for it." And while you're waiting, don't make the mistake of trying to figure everything out. "God, I've been praying for my child for three years. Why won't he change?" If you're constantly trying to figure things out, that's only going to frustrate you. Turn it over to God. Say with David, "God, my times are in Your hands. I'm not going to worry about why something hasn't happened or why it's taking so long. God, I trust You. I know at the set time everything You promised me will come to pass."

Doors Will Open

A couple of years after my father died, I really wanted to write a book. I had a strong desire, but I didn't know any publishers or anything about the book industry. Several times I started to call a friend who did know a publisher, but I didn't feel good about it. I knew it wasn't right. Over the next couple of years, I was approached by different publishers and even offered a contract. On the surface it looked good. They were fine people, but inside I could hear a still, small voice telling me, "Joel, be patient. This is not the right one. Trust My timing. Something better is coming."

I put it on hold month after month. I didn't worry about it. I wasn't frustrated. My attitude was, *God, my times are in Your hands. When You want me to write a book, I know You will open up the doors.*

You can do the right thing at the wrong time and miss God's best. Timing is everything. Be patient and let God open the doors. You may have to knock. You'll have to put forth the effort. I'm a believer in being aggressive and pursuing dreams, but you don't have to force doors to open. You don't have to try to make people like you. You don't have to talk yourself into it. If you'll be patient and wait for God's timing, He will *give* you the desires of your heart.

> *You can do the right thing at the wrong time and miss God's best.*

One day through a series of unusual events, I met this publisher. I knew they were the right people. I felt good about it. Everything fell into place. And that book, *Your Best Life Now*, went on to become a huge success and has been published in many languages. That's what happens when you wait for God's timing.

Be Still and Know

This principle is especially important when we're facing challenges. If you get a negative medical report, if you lose your biggest client at the office, or if somebody at work is talking behind your back and try-ing to make you look bad, it's easy to get all wrought up and think, *I have to get in there and straighten things out. I'm going to fix that person. I have to get a second job. I'll never make it without that client.*

So often we think we have to do it only in our own strength. This is when many people make quick decisions that end up only making matters worse. The Scripture says, "Be still and know that I am God." When you feel overwhelmed and you're tempted to take everything into your own hands, you have to make yourself be still. The battle is not yours. The battle is the Lord's. But as long as you're fighting it, trying to make it happen your way, trying to pay some-body back, upset, worried, then God is going to step back and let you do it on your own. But when you take it out of your hands and say, "God, I trust You. I know You have already set the time to bring me out. You've already set the time to vindicate me. You've set the time to bring healing. So I'm going to be still and know that You are God," that's when God will fight your battles.

This is what the Israelites did. They were surrounded by a huge army and greatly outnumbered. They were so worried and stressed out. They were getting their equipment on, trying to come up with some type of strategy to fight off the enemy. Just before they went to battle, they decided to pray. God said to them, "Stand still, and you will see the deliverance of the Lord. For the Lord will fight for you, if you remain at rest."

Notice the condition. God will turn it around. God will restore you. God will vindicate you, *if you will be still and remain at rest.* In other words, if you will wait for the set time, if you will be patient and not give birth to Ishmaels, then God has Isaacs in your future.

Maybe you're facing a big challenge. You can't sleep well at night. You're upset and frustrated. God is saying to you what He said to them, "Be still. I have it all figured out. I control the whole universe. I've already set the time to deliver you. I've already set the time to not only bring you out, but to bring you out better off than you were before."

Now do your part and rest. Trust God's timing. God knows what He is doing. We may not understand why something is taking so long, but sometimes God will delay an answer on purpose simply so He can show His power in a greater way.

When Pharaoh wouldn't let the Israelites go, God had Moses tell him that if Pharaoh didn't change his mind, God was going to send plague after plague on Pharaoh and his people. The Scripture says that "God caused Pharaoh to harden his heart." It wasn't the enemy. God caused him to be stubborn and not give in.

Moses warned, "Pharaoh, if you don't let us go, God is going to send locusts that are going to eat all your crops and destroy the food supply."

Pharaoh replied, "I don't care. Let Him do it. I'm not changing my mind."

One bad plague after another, and he wouldn't give in. Why? God wanted to show His power in a greater way. When all those plagues were harming Pharaoh and his people, not one plague affected the Israelites living in that same area.

Everything Promised Will Come to Pass

Your situation may be taking longer than you thought. Maybe it's something more difficult than you've ever experienced. That doesn't mean that the enemy is getting the best of you. It doesn't mean that God went on vacation and is not concerned anymore. Just as with Pharaoh, God has not turned it around yet because He wants to show His favor in your life in an amazing way. God is going to show His strength, His healing, His goodness, and His power like you've never seen before. You might as well get ready. When God brings you out, everybody around you is going to have no doubt that the God you serve is an awesome God.

My challenge is, trust God's timing. Stand still, and you'll see God deliver you. When you remain at rest, Almighty God will fight your battles. Friend, there are set times in your future. Quit worrying about when it's going to happen. God can see the big picture. He knows what's best for you. Dare to say with David, "God, my times are in Your hand." When you do this, it takes all the pressure off. You don't have to struggle and try to force things to happen. You know God has it all figured out. So you can relax and enjoy your life while you're waiting for the promises to come to pass. If you will enter into this rest, trusting God's timing, because you have faith and patience, I believe and declare, you're going to come into set times of favor, set times of healing, set times of promotion, and set times of breakthrough. God is going to give you the desires of your heart. Everything He has promised you will come to pass.

> *God is going to give you the desires of your heart.*

I AM
FORGIVEN

CHAPTER SEVENTEEN

God Loves Imperfect People

Most of the time we believe God loves us as long as we're making good decisions, resisting temptation, and treating people right. We know God is on our side. But the problem with this kind of reasoning is that we all make mistakes. No matter how good a person you are, there will be times when you don't perform perfectly, times when you have doubts, times when you fail. You know you should bite your tongue, but you told them off anyway. You said it would be the last time, but you gave into compromise once again. When we don't perform perfectly, it's easy to think that God is far from us. "I blew it. God would never have anything to do with me."

I have people ask me all the time, "Joel, will you pray for me? I know God would never hear my prayers, not with the life I've lived, the mistakes I've made." I say this respectfully, but sometimes religion pushes people down. It says, "If you turn your back on God, He will turn His back on you. If you make poor choices, don't expect God to bail you out. It was your own fault." But the truth is that when you fall, God

> *When you fall, God doesn't turn away from you. He comes running toward you.*

doesn't turn away from you. He comes running toward you. When you blow it, God doesn't say, "Too bad. You had your chance." He comes after you with a greater passion.

I heard somebody say, "When you make a mistake, God doesn't love you the same. He loves you a little bit more, so much so that He pursues you. He will turn up the intensity. He won't leave you alone until He sees you restored and back on the right course." In other words, God will express His love in a greater way. He will send people across your path to encourage you, to help reignite your faith. Or maybe when you're out walking through the neighborhood, you hear the church bells ringing. You feel a warmness inside. That's the mercy of God coming after you, saying, "You may have blown it, but you're still My child. You may have let Me down, but I'm not going to let you down. You may have lost faith in Me, but I haven't lost faith in you."

We don't have to have a perfect performance where we never have a doubt or make a mistake. Certainly, we should try our best each day to honor God. But what I'm saying is, don't beat yourself up if you don't perform perfectly all the time. God loves imperfect people.

When Peter Failed the Worst

Think about Peter. Before Jesus chose him to become a disciple, Jesus knew that Peter would deny Him, but He chose him anyway. God knows every mistake that we will ever make. All of our days have been written in His book from the beginning to the end. God knows every time you will fail, every time you take the easy way out, and every time you will lose your temper. The good news is, God still chose you. He still says, "That's My child," and He will still help you fulfill your destiny. Why? Because God's love is not based on our performance. It's based on our relationship. We are His children.

When Jesus was about to be crucified, He said to Peter, "You will deny Me three times before the rooster crows tonight."

Peter said, "No, Jesus. I'm your most faithful disciple. I'll stick with You through thick and thin to the very end."

They arrested Jesus. Peter was watching it all take place from a distance. A young lady came over and pointed at Peter and said, "He is one of His followers. I've seen this man with Jesus."

Peter said, "No, ma'am. You've got it wrong. You're mistaken. I don't know the man." He denied Him once. It happened a second time. The third time the girl came over even more emphatically and said to the guards, "I know he is one of His followers. I'm certain that I have seen this man with Jesus."

This time Peter got upset, started cursing, swearing. "Girl, what are you talking about? You're making all this up. I've never seen the man." Right on cue, the rooster crowed.

Jesus looked over at Peter. Their eyes met. You can imagine how Peter must have felt. When Jesus needed him the most, when He was at His lowest moment, He needed a friend to stick up for Him, but Peter didn't do it. The Scripture says, "Peter went out and wept bitterly." He felt ashamed. No doubt he was beating himself up, thinking, *Peter, what is wrong with you? How could you be such a coward?*

Not long after that, they crucified Jesus. Peter never had a chance to make things right. He never had the chance to say, "Jesus, I'm sorry. I blew it. I promise You that I'll be there for You next time." He had to carry the guilt and heaviness of betraying his friend, the Messiah, whom he dearly loved.

We've all made mistakes. We've all failed. But none of us have failed as big as Peter. None of us has denied Christ when He needed us the most, when

> *We've all made mistakes. But none of us have failed as big as Peter.*

He was about to be crucified. You would think that Peter would have missed his destiny. Surely God wouldn't have anything to do with him. No; when you make a mistake, God doesn't turn away from you. He turns toward you. He doesn't love you less. He loves you more. He comes after you.

They crucified Jesus on Friday. On Sunday morning, Mary Magdalene went to the tomb to check on His body. When she arrived, she noticed that the stone was rolled away. She went in, and an angel appeared and said, "Mary, don't be afraid. Jesus is not here. He is risen. Now go tell His disciples and Peter that He is alive."

Out of all the people in the world God could have mentioned at this historic time, the only person He specifically pointed out was Peter. God was saying, "Peter, I know you think I'm disappointed in you, and I'll never have anything to do with you. But Peter, that's not who I am. I'm the God of another chance. When you fall, I come running toward you. When you turn your back on Me, I don't turn My back on you."

God is saying to all the people who have fallen, the people who have made mistakes, "I'm not only alive, but I still love you. I still believe in you. If you will let go of the guilt and move forward, I will still get you to where you are supposed to be."

Now you have to do your part and receive God's mercy. If Peter would have listened to the accusing voices and gone around beating himself up, he would have gotten stuck where he was. I can imagine that when he heard Mary say, "Peter, the angel specifically said to tell you that Jesus is alive," he said, "Mary, did He really call my name?" "Yes. He said, 'Tell Peter.'" When Peter heard that, something ignited inside him. He shook off the guilt, shook off the self-pity, and said, "I may have blown it in the past, but that doesn't have to keep me from my future. I'm still going to become who God has created me to be."

Not long after that, Peter went out and ministered, and three thousand people came to know the Lord—the most ever recorded in the Scripture. It would have never happened if Peter hadn't understood this principle: God doesn't write us off when we make mistakes. God doesn't cancel our destiny because we've taken a few detours. Maybe today you're down on yourself because you're not where you thought you would be in life. You've made some poor choices. Now you're letting the guilt weigh you down. That heaviness is keeping you from God's best. Just as God specifically called Peter's name, He is calling your name today, saying, "Tell John, tell William, tell Ricardo, tell Shannon, tell Maria, I have forgiven them. I am not disappointed in them. I am not withholding My blessing. I still have an amazing future in front of them." God is calling your name today. He is running toward you.

God's Mercies Are Always Greater

In the Scripture, it talks about the God of Abraham, the God of Isaac, and the God of Jacob. I can understand how He is the God of Abraham. After all, Abraham is the father of our faith. I can understand how He is the God of Isaac. Isaac was extremely obedient, even willing to be sacrificed. But when it says He is the God of Jacob, that doesn't make a lot of sense. Jacob was a cheater. He went around deceiving people. He stole his brother's birthright. Jacob was known for making poor choices. Yet God is called the God of Abraham, Isaac, and Jacob. What was God saying? "I'm not just the God of perfect people. I'm not just the God of people who never make a mistake. I'm the God of people who have failed. I'm the God of people who have blown

> *When it says He is the God of Jacob, that doesn't make a lot of sense. Jacob went around deceiving people.*

it. I'm the God of people who have had a rough past."

It's interesting that later in Jacob's life, he changed his ways. He got his life straightened out. God changed his name from Jacob to

Israel. That was to signify his new beginning. God could have been known as the God of Abraham, Isaac, and Israel. That seems to make more sense. That was his new name, once he was restored and redeemed. But God on purpose left it as the God of Abraham, Isaac, and Jacob to forever settle it that "I'm not just the God of perfect people. I'm the God of imperfect people, too."

You may have made mistakes, but be encouraged. He is the God of Jacob. He is still your God. You may have lost your temper, struggled with an addiction, or compromised your integrity. Don't beat yourself up. He is the God of Jacob. He is your God, too.

In the book of John, there was a lady who had been married five times. She was living with a sixth man. You could imagine the heartache and pain that she had gone through. I'm sure she felt beaten down by life—not really living, just existing.

Jesus was about to travel to another city and told His disciples, "I must go through Samaria."

They said, "Jesus, that's the long way. There's a shortcut, a much quicker route." They tried to talk Him out of it.

He replied, "No, you don't understand. I must go through Samaria. There's a woman there who feels condemned. She is about to give up on life. I must go express My love. I have to encourage her, get her back on the right course."

She is known as "The Woman at the Well." It's interesting that the first person Jesus revealed Himself to as the Messiah was not the religious leaders. It was not the priests and the rabbis in the synagogue. It was this woman; a woman who had made mistakes, a woman who was beaten down by life—an imperfect person. That one encounter changed her life.

But too many people, like her, are sitting on the sidelines of life. They feel as though they've blown it too many times. They've failed, and they haven't measured up. Now they're letting the accusing voices convince them that they're all washed up. God is disappointed in them. "You can't expect God's favor." You have to get this truth down into your spirit: You may have made mistakes, but God is not running from you. He is running to you. He doesn't love you less. He loves you more. He is expressing His love to you today. You wouldn't be reading this if God wasn't reaching out to you.

Get rid of the guilt, shake off the condemnation, quit thinking about what could have or should have been, and get back in the game. You're not supposed to sit on the sidelines. God is not disappointed in you. Nothing you have done is a surprise to God. Do your part and start moving forward. You can still fulfill your destiny. God's mercy is bigger than any mistake that you've made.

> *Get rid of the guilt, shake off the condemnation, quit thinking about what could have or should have been, and get back in the game.*

Don't Mix Your Performance with Your Identity

The Scripture talks about how God searches the earth to show Himself strong in people whose hearts are turned perfect toward Him. It doesn't say that God is looking for a perfect performance. God is looking for people who have a heart that is turned perfect toward Him. That means if you get up each day with a desire to please God, if down deep you really want to honor Him, then like Peter, you will have times that you fail. You wanted to resist, but you gave in. The good news is that does not cancel your destiny. Your performance may not be perfect, but because your heart is perfect toward God, He still has something amazing in your future.

No matter what you've done, don't go around beating yourself up. You can't change the past. Learn from your mistakes, but don't get stuck there. Keep moving forward. Receive God's mercy. Be bold enough to say, "God, I blew it. I know I was wrong. I should have done better. But God, I know You are not holding it against me. I know You are not just the God of Abraham. You are the God of Jacob, too—the God of imperfect people."

When Thomas heard that Jesus had risen from the grave and people had seen him alive, everyone was so excited—except Thomas. He was more practical and more logical. He said, "Guys, if you want to believe, that's fine, but not me. A man can't be dead for three days and come back to life. I'm not going to believe unless I see it with my own eyes. I want to see the nail prints in His hands." Thomas had spent just as much time with Jesus as the other disciples, yet they were full of faith. They were all believers. Thomas was full of doubt. He had all these questions.

One day they were in a room together, and Jesus came walking *through* the doors. They nearly passed out. What's interesting is Jesus didn't go over to Andrew and say, "Andrew, I made it." He didn't walk over to Matthew and give him a big hug. Jesus walked right to Thomas, bypassed all the people who had faith, and went to the one person in the room who had doubt. He didn't chew him out and say, "Thomas, what's wrong with you?" He said, "Thomas, I know you don't believe. I know you have doubts. You have questions. And Thomas, that's okay. I understand. That's why I came to you first. Now feel the nail prints in My hands. Feel the scars in My side."

Notice the pattern. When you have doubts as Thomas did, when you blow it as Peter did, when you fail as the woman who was married five times did, you think God is far away from you. It's just the opposite. God came to the people who had doubt before He came to the people who had faith. We try to put God in a box and tell Him who to save and who to bless and who to forgive and who to heal.

The longer I live, the more I realize God's ways are not our ways. God will save the most unlikely people. He will show mercy when we think they deserve judgment.

Thomas doubted this one time, yet he became known as "Doubting Thomas." It probably wasn't a week or two of his life, but people labeled him a doubter. The good news is God doesn't judge you by one mistake. We call him Doubting Thomas. You know what God calls him? Believing Thomas, Forgiven Thomas, Redeemed Thomas, Restored Thomas, Amazing Thomas. What we don't hear much about is that Thomas went on to touch all of India. He is credited as being the one who brought the Good News to that entire nation.

You may have struggled with an addiction your whole life, but know this: God is not judging you by that one setback. Get rid of that negative label. Maybe you've failed in business, blown a relationship, done something you're not proud of. Don't let that become your identity. Stop seeing yourself as Doubting Thomas, Addicted Thomas, Undisciplined Thomas, Failing Thomas. You have to turn it around. Start seeing yourself as Blessed Thomas, Free Thomas, Redeemed Thomas, Successful Thomas. Dare to declare it: "I am forgiven. I am redeemed."

Too often we get our performance mixed up with our identity. You may have failed, but you are not a failure. That's what you did. Failure is an event. That's not who you are. You are a child of the Most High God. You've been handpicked by the Creator of the universe. You may struggle with an addiction, but you

> *Too often we get our performance mixed up with our identity.*

are not an addict. That's what you did. That's not who you are. You are free. You are clean. You are restored.

Quit Replaying Your Failures

Don't go around dwelling on your past mistakes. Quit replaying all the times that you've failed, the times you gave in to temptation, the time you blew the relationship, the time it didn't work out. All that's going to do is depress you. Just like you have a remote control to change the channel on the television, you have to change the channel in your mind. You will not be free from guilt or enjoy your life if you are constantly replaying the negative memories of your past. If you're going to replay anything, replay your victories. Replay the time that you honored God. Replay the times that you helped someone else in need. That will change your perspective.

A few years ago a young lady named Rachel Smith won the Miss USA beauty pageant. She is a bright young girl who goes all over the world helping underprivileged children. Later that year, she competed in the Miss Universe pageant. As she walked out on stage during the evening gown competition, all by herself, with millions of people watching around the world, on live television, she lost her footing and fell flat on her backside. She was embarrassed, but she got up as quickly as she could and put a smile back on her face. The audience wasn't very forgiving. There were jeers and laughter and boos, which was very humiliating. In spite of the fall, she made it into the top five of the competition. Her next task was to answer a question randomly chosen by the judges. She walked back onto the stage where she had fallen just a few minutes earlier. A judge picked a question out of the hat. Her question was, "If you could relive any moment of your life over again and do it differently, what moment would that be?"

Her most embarrassing moment was just twenty minutes earlier. How many of us would say, "I want to redo that. I want to relive that"? But without missing a beat, she said, "If I could relive any moment of my life again, I would relive my trip to Africa, working with the orphans, seeing their beautiful smiles, feeling their warm embraces." Instead of reliving a moment of pain, a moment of embarrassment, she chose to relive a moment of joy, a moment when she was making a difference, when she was proud of herself.

In life, we're all going to have times where we fall, embarrassing moments, unfair situations. I can assure you they will come up on the movie screen of your mind again and again. You have to

> *You have to get good at changing the channel. Put on your accomplishments. Put on your victories.*

get good at changing the channel. Put on your accomplishments. Put on your victories. Put on the times when you've been proud of yourself.

Shake Off the Guilt

Friend, your sins have already been forgiven. Every mistake you've made and ever will make has already been paid in full. The real question is, will you receive God's mercy? You don't have to go around feeling guilty, feeling wrong inside, not excited about your future. God is running toward you today. He knew every mistake you would ever make. He doesn't love you less. He loves you more. He's not just the God of Abraham; He's the God of Jacob. He is saying, "You may have blown it. You may have failed. But I'm not disappointed in you. I still love you. I still believe in you. I still have an amazing future in front of you."

Your performance may not have been perfect, but because your heart is perfect toward Him, God is going to show Himself strong in your behalf. If you'll shake off the guilt and receive God's mercy, you will not only live freer, but you will still become all you were created to be.

I AM
PROTECTED

CHAPTER EIGHTEEN

You've Been Framed

We've all heard the phrase, *you've been framed*. Most of the time we think of it as a bad thing. We've been set up, made to look as though we did something that we didn't do. But the Scripture talks about a different type of frame. It says, "The worlds were framed by the Word of God." It's not just talking about the physical *worlds*. The word in the original language is *eons*, meaning "ages" or "times." It's saying that God has a frame around your times. He has put a fence, a boundary, around your life. Nothing can penetrate your frame that God doesn't allow. Trouble, sickness, accidents—they can't just randomly happen. The frame is set.

You don't have to worry about your future. There's a frame around your health, a frame around your children, and a frame around your finances. It's a boundary set by the Creator of the universe. Not only can nothing get in without God's permission, but even better news, you can't get out. You can't make a mistake big enough to break out of that frame. You can't get too addicted, too discouraged, too angry. It's a destiny frame. God won't let you get so far off course that you can't still fulfill your purpose. You may come right up to the edge and be about to do something to get yourself in trouble, but you'll bump into the frame. God will push you right back.

I had a man tell me how he was so fed up with his boss. He had worked at the company for many years. His boss was always condescending, making sarcastic remarks, and this man had had all he could take. He was about to give his boss a piece of his mind. He knew he'd get fired, but at this point he didn't care. As he lay in bed the night before, he had his speech all lined up and was steaming over it, thinking, *I'm going to tell him, "I don't like you. I don't need you. You're a lousy boss."* On and on. He was going to let it all hang out.

The first thing the next morning, he marched into his boss's office without knocking, all fired up. Then the strangest thing happened. He got flustered. He couldn't remember what he was going to say. His mind totally went blank. He looked at the boss and said, "Uh...uh...uh...would you like a cup of coffee?" He told me later, "Joel, I tried to tell him off. I tried to be mean. I just couldn't do it." What happened? He bumped into the frame. God knows how to protect you, not only from accidents, not only from the wrong people. God will protect you from yourself. Sometimes we're the most dangerous thing we face.

> Sometimes we're the most dangerous thing we face.

At the family reunion, you're about to tell your relative off. Somehow you feel a peace come over you. Or they walk out of the room at just the right time. That's not a coincidence. You'd better thank God for your frame.

Out on the freeway, that person who cut you off, you're about to give them a signal with your hand. And I'm not talking about, "One

Way Jesus." You pull up next to them so aggravated, throw your hand up, but instead of doing what you thought, you just smile and give them a big friendly wave.

What happened? You bumped into your frame. This frame has kept us out of more trouble than we realize. You'd better thank God for your frame or you might not still have a job. If it had not been for the frame, you might not still be married. How many times were we going to tell our spouse exactly what we thought, and exactly what they should do, and we hear the still, small voice saying, "Don't do it. Bite your tongue. Walk away." We take the advice. That's the frame.

The Right Person at the Right Time

In the Scripture, David experienced this frame. He and his men had been protecting a wealthy man by the name of Nabal who had thousands of sheep. They were camped next door. Just to do him a favor, they made sure that no bandits bothered him or his property. One day David asked his men to go ask Nabal for some food. Nabal was very rude and an evil man. He told those men, "I don't owe you anything. I didn't ask you to do this. Get off my property!"

When David heard what Nabal had said, he was furious. He told his men, "Pack up. We're going to go wipe out Nabal and anyone that's halfway associated with him." This set David off. As he headed toward Nabal's house, angry, offended, and ready to take vengeance, God sent a young lady named Abigail, who was Nabal's wife, to intercept David before he struck. She met David on the road with gifts and food.

Abigail said, "David, you are called to be our next king. You are destined to do great things. My husband, Nabal, is a fool. Why are you going to waste your time fighting with him? You could miss your destiny." She spoke sense into him.

David replied, "You're exactly right," turned around, and went back home.

You know what Abigail was? She was a part of the frame. God ordained her to be there at the right time, to know exactly the right thing to say. Had David gotten distracted, killed Nabal and all his men, caused a big stir by shedding innocent blood, that mistake could have kept him from taking the throne. David went right up to the edge, but he bumped into his frame.

> *The right person will show up to say the right thing to keep you from missing your destiny.*

God is so good. He will always send the right person to say the right thing to keep you from missing your destiny. David said, "Where would I be without the goodness of God?" He could have said, "Where would I be without this frame?"

Even When We Run the Opposite Way

Jonah experienced the frame. God told him to go to the city of Nineveh, but he didn't want to go there. He said, "God, that's what You want me to do. I want to go my own way." He went in the opposite direction. God will always let you do your own thing. He'll let you go your own way, but He is so merciful—at some point, you're going to bump into your frame. He let Jonah go the wrong direction. Jonah ended up on a ship out at sea in the middle of a huge storm. He finally told the crew that he was the problem. This crew had no mercy. They said, "Jonah, you're the problem. Good riddance. You're out of here." They threw him overboard.

You would think this would be the end of Jonah's life. He brought the trouble on himself. He knew the right thing, but he did the opposite. He had nobody to blame except himself. I'm sure Jonah felt that he was finished. He said his good-byes, made his peace, and down he went. But what Jonah didn't realize was the frame God had put around his life. Yes, he made a mistake, but it wasn't outside the frame. Yes, he was in trouble, but that trouble wasn't a surprise to God. God allowed the difficulty into Jonah's frame not to harm him but to push him toward his divine destiny. When things looked hopeless to Jonah, when he was out in the sea treading water with no chance to survive, along comes a big fish and swallows him. You know what the fish was? As Abigail was to David's frame, the fish was part of Jonah's frame. Three days later that fish spit him out onto dry ground. Jonah said, "You know what? I think I'll go to Nineveh after all."

As Jonah did, you can run as much as you want, but the good news is you'll never run out of your frame. You'll keep bumping up against it again and again. It will always push you back toward your divine destiny. In other words, you can go out and party, live it up, not give God the time of day. But while your friends are partying, while they're enjoying life, deep down you'll be miserable, thinking, *Why can't I enjoy this? Why am I so unsatisfied?* It's because of the frame God has put on your life. You are ruined for living a defeated, mediocre, compromising life. God's calling is on you. You can go your own way, but God has a way of getting you back on course.

God has built a frame that you can't penetrate. The enemy can't penetrate. Drugs can't penetrate. The wrong people can't penetrate.

> *You can run from the call. You can try to ignore it. But the frame around your life was put in place before the foundation of time.*

The Most High God has fenced you in. He has put boundaries around your life so strong that all the forces of darkness cannot get in and you cannot get out. And yes, you can make mistakes. You can run from the call. You can try to ignore it. But the frame around your life was put in place before the foundation of time. When God breathed His life into you, He framed your world.

Even When Our Children Make Bad Choices

That's why, parents, we don't have to worry about our children. They've been framed. They may get off course, but sooner or later they'll bump into the frame. They may run with the wrong crowd, but the frame is up. They can't go too far to miss their destiny. They're going to bump into it again, again, and again, until they finally say, "I'm tired of fighting. God, I'm going to let You have Your way. I'm going to honor You with my life."

Some of you, because you had a praying mother, or a praying grandmother, or you had relatives who honored God, you might as well give up. You don't have a chance. Your frame is so set. You're going to keep bumping into it until God gets you to where you're supposed to be.

I know a mother who was so concerned about her son. He was making very poor choices. She tried to convince him to quit running with the wrong crowd and to come to church. He just wouldn't do it. He ended up in jail. One Sunday morning he was watching television in the common area. Another inmate came in and wanted to watch something different. They started arguing and ended up in a struggle for the remote control, trying to get it out of each other's hands.

About that time a huge inmate, who looked like a professional football player, walked in. Six foot six, with muscles bulging out of his shirt, he grabbed the remote control and said, "Give me that thing. I'll decide what we're going to watch." He started flipping through the channels and came across our program. He said, "We're going to watch Joel today." The other two inmates got up to leave, but he grabbed the one young man by the shirt and pulled him back down and said, "Sit down. You're going to watch with me." What happened? He bumped into the frame. A really big frame, I might add.

Parents, God has the right people not only lined up for you, but also for your children, for your grandchildren. Quit worrying about them and start thanking God for the frame. Don't ever go around telling your friends how your children are so off course, and they're never going to do what's right. No, zip that up and get in agreement with God. "Lord, I want to thank You that my children have been framed. I've committed them into Your hands. And Lord, You said the seed of the righteous will be mighty in the land."

As the inmate was watching the program with this six-foot-six inmate making sure he watched, he began to feel God's presence. He started weeping. Right there in the jail, that big inmate led him to Christ. Now I see this young man at our services all the time sitting next to his mother.

You may not see how it can happen. That's not your job. Your job is to stay in peace, knowing that your children have been framed. Your prayers are activating God's power. When you pray, just imagine the frame is getting smaller, the boundaries are getting tighter.

God won't let them go as far as they used to. He will make them uncomfortable in compromising situations. He won't let them enjoy doing wrong as they did before. God knows how to tighten the frame.

When I was nineteen years old, I was driving home from a ball game very late at night. There was nobody on the freeway. I had a sports car. The fastest I had driven it was about seventy-five miles an hour. I thought, *This would be a great time to see how fast this car will really go.* It was one o'clock in the morning, five lanes of freeway in front of me. I was on the top of a big bridge and could see about two miles down the road. There was hardly anybody on the road, just a car or two here and there, so I put the pedal to the floor and my car took off going very fast. I'm not going to tell you how fast, because my mother will read this!

But as I was flying down the highway, feeling so cool, I looked over and there was a car right next to me. I thought, *I can't believe it. He wants to race. He can't race me. He's got a piece of junk.* So I pushed the gas pedal down even farther, took off, and shot ahead. When I looked over, there he was again, but this time when I looked, he was holding up his badge. I nearly went to Heaven right then and there. My heart stopped. I looked back over, and he mouthed the words, "Slow down!" I drove thirty miles an hour the rest of the way home.

Parents, God has a frame around your children. Even when they do dumb things, they can't get out of the frame. God will always have the right person, whether it's Abigail, a six-foot-six inmate, or an off-duty police officer going down the freeway at one in the morning. We can't get out of the frame.

Even When We Kick Against
the Frame

In the Scripture there was a man named Saul. He was the biggest enemy of the church. He hated believers. He was having them put in prison, doing more harm to God's people than any person of that time. One day he was on the road traveling to Damascus and a bright light shone down on him, so bright that he fell to the ground and became blind. The voice said, "Saul, why do you persecute Me? Don't you know it's hard to kick against the pricks?" God was saying, "Saul, I have you in My frame. You're trying to kick, trying to run, trying to ignore it. But Saul, you have to understand that I set the frame. I have a destiny for you to fulfill, and it's not to stop My work. It's to advance My work." Lying on the ground, not able to see, Saul asked, "Who are you?" The voice boomed out, "I am Jesus, whom you persecute." Notice, when people persecute you, give you a hard time for honoring God, or make fun of you for going to church, don't let that bother you. They're not really doing it to you. They're doing it unto God. Saul was harming believers, yet God said, "You're persecuting Me." God took it personally. The voice told Saul to go to the city and see Ananias, who prayed for Saul. He got his sight back. Saul became the Apostle Paul, who went on to write over half of the books of the New Testament.

You may think that you're too far gone and have made too many mistakes. People tell me often, "Joel, I'm just not a religious person." But none of that matters. All that matters is that the Creator of the universe has put a frame around your life. You can kick, run, and try to ignore it. That's just going to make you more miserable. As God said to Saul, it's hard to keep kicking against the frame. The frame is not going to move. There is a calling on your life, a destiny for you to fulfill. It has been set there by the Most High God. The Scripture talks about how God's calling is irrevocable. God is not going to remove the frame. It's wise if you just surrender and say, "God, my life is in Your hands. I'm going to live for You. I'm going to get rid of these friends who are pulling me down. I'm going to get help with these bad habits. I'm going to get in church and serve and grow. I'm going to pursue the dreams You have placed in my heart." The sooner you do that, the happier and the more fulfilling your life will be.

You may have family members or friends like Saul. You've been praying for them a long time. It doesn't look like they'll ever get on course. In fact, the more you pray, the worse they get. Don't get discouraged. Stay in peace. Just as Saul was, they've been framed.

A Hedge of Protection

A part of this frame is a hedge of protection. God has a boundary around your life that the enemy cannot cross. A friend of mine was driving home from work the other day and stopped at a light. When it changed to green, he cautiously looked to the left and to the right. As he was about to go forward, something said to him very strongly, "Look again!" He looked back to the right a second time. A car was coming full speed, never attempted to stop, and ran right through the red light. If he had not looked that second time, he would have gotten broadsided. There's no telling what would have happened.

What was that? The frame. If it's not your time to go, the enemy cannot take you out. The frame that's placed around your life was put there by the most powerful force in the universe. That's why the psalmist said, "A thousand may fall at my side, ten thousand at my right hand. I'm not worried. It can't come near me. I know there's a frame around my life. Nothing can happen without God's permission."

> The frame that's placed around your life was put there by the most powerful force in the universe.

I had somebody complaining to me once about how they were hit on the freeway. It totaled their car. They were upset and discouraged. They didn't know if the insurance was going to cover it. It was a brand-new car. The feeling I got from them was that God had let them down. They said, "If I have this frame, how come I had an accident?" Keep the right perspective. You may have lost your car, but because of the frame, you didn't lose your life. Because of the frame, you're not paralyzed. Because of the frame, you can still see and talk and hear. I'm convinced, God protects us from so many things that we don't even realize. We think sometimes, *I didn't have anything good happen to me. Just an average week.* You can thank God for what didn't happen. Because of the frame, you didn't have an accident. Because of the frame, you're not in the hospital. Because of the frame, you didn't get laid off. Because of the frame, your children are still healthy and whole.

A few years ago I was in San Antonio at Brooke Army Medical Center, praying for some of our soldiers. This hospital specializes in treating people who have burns. I left one room, and a couple stopped me and asked me to go in and pray for their son who had been badly burned when he was a soldier in Iraq. In the middle of the night, he had been on the army base refueling the large tanks of gas. He was all alone about a mile from the main area when something caused the tanks to ignite. When he woke up, he was twenty yards away, flat on his back, on fire, unable to move. He was wearing ammunition that could explode at any moment. Out of nowhere two Iraqi civilian men showed up and started rolling him in the dirt to stop the fire. Without those two men, he certainly would have burned to death. What's interesting is that those men were not allowed on the base. They were in a secure area at three o'clock in the morning. The parents said, "Those men had to have been put there by God to save our son." What was that? The frame. It wasn't his time to go. The enemy doesn't determine your destiny. God does. God is bigger than an explosion, bigger than an accident, bigger than a car running a red light. God has you in a frame.

Even Death Cannot Penetrate Our Frame

When I was ten years old, our family went to Hawaii. We arrived about three o'clock in the afternoon and were so excited. After our parents checked us into the hotel, all five of us children ran down to the beach to go swimming. My brother, Paul, and sister Lisa were in their late teens, and they were supposed to watch over us. We rented some floats and took off into the waves. But in the excitement of playing in the big waves and having so much fun, we looked up and couldn't find my eight-year-old sister, April. We searched and searched frantically—five minutes, ten minutes, twenty minutes, thirty minutes. I had never felt such a sick feeling in all my life. We were sure April had drowned. The waves were huge. We searched for forty-five minutes, then an hour; still nothing. An hour and fifteen minutes later, we saw April way, way down the beach, walking toward us, carrying her float. We had never been so happy and so mad at her at the same time.

April had fallen asleep on that float. It was six hours later at home, about eleven o'clock at night, and she was tired. She drifted nearly two miles down the shore. She could have drifted out to sea. She could have woken up in deep water and not been able to swim in it. A thousand things could have happened, but God had her in a frame. There was a boundary set around her.

Let me assure you, death can't penetrate your frame. God has to allow it. The number of your days, He will fulfill. That's why I always tell people who have lost a loved one, especially if they went home at an early age, while we may not understand it, know this: The enemy didn't take your loved one. He doesn't have that power. God called them home. God received them into His presence. The angels carried them into the Heavenly Father's arms.

When Jesus rose from the grave, He said, "You don't have to worry anymore. I hold the keys of death." He was saying, "Nobody determines your time except Me."

Death can't penetrate your frame. An accident can't penetrate your frame. Sickness can't penetrate your frame. God has to give it permission. He controls the whole universe. When you understand this, you can say with the Apostle Paul, "O death, where is your sting? O grave, where is your victory? I'm not afraid of you. You can't defeat me. I know there is a frame around my life. I'm not worried about my health. I've been framed. I'm not afraid to drive on the freeway. A thousand may fall at my side. That's okay. I have a frame. Ten thousand at my right hand. No problem. I've been framed. It's a hedge of protection, a bloodline that the enemy cannot cross."

> *Death can't penetrate your frame. An accident can't penetrate your frame. Sickness can't penetrate your frame.*

We see this principle in Job's life. Satan was looking for somebody to test. God said to Satan, "Have you seen my servant, Job? There's none like him in all the land."

Satan answered back something interesting. He said, "Yes, God, I've seen Job, but You know I can't touch him. You've put a hedge around him. You've got a frame around his life." He went on to say, "If You will remove the frame and let me get to him, he'll curse You."

What I want you to see is the enemy can't just do whatever he wants. He has to ask God for permission. God has to allow him to do it. Job went through a time of testing. He fought the good fight. And in the end, not only did he not curse God, but he came out with double what he had before.

When you go through tough times, if you have a bad break, if you're facing a sickness, don't get discouraged. Remember, the frame is still up. You keep moving forward, and you'll not only come out, but as Job did, God will bring you out better off than you were before.

You Will Fulfill Your Destiny

Friend, don't worry about your future. You've been framed. There are boundaries around your life put in place by the most powerful force in the universe. Not only can nothing get in without God's permission, you can't get out. You may run as Jonah did, but there'll be a fish waiting for you. You may kick, as Saul did, but before long you'll be the Apostle Paul. You may be about to take vengeance on somebody, as David was. Don't worry. Abigail is going to show up. That's the frame.

Now, all through the day, instead of worrying, instead of being stressed out, under your breath, say, "Lord, thank You that my life has been framed. Thank You that my children are framed. Lord, thank You that my health, my finances, my dreams, and my future are in Your frame. I am protected."

If you'll do that, you'll not only be happier, you'll not only have more peace, but God promises the number of your days He will fulfill. You will see His protection, His mercy, and His favor. And nothing will keep you from your God-given destiny.

I AM
GENEROUS

CHAPTER NINETEEN

Become a Miracle

Many people are praying for a miracle. They're saying, "God, please send me a friend. God, I need help with these children. I need training. God, I need a good break." We have to realize that we can become the miracle they need. God uses people. He has no hands to heal except through our hands. He has no voice to encourage except through our voice. He has no arms to hug except through our arms. God will bring people across our path so that we can be the answer to their prayer.

You may not realize it, but you are a miracle waiting to happen. Somebody you know is lonely. They're praying for a friend. You're the miracle that they're waiting for. Somebody got a bad medical report. They're worried and praying, "God, please send me a sign. Let me know that You're still in control." You are that sign. A simple phone call to say, "I'm thinking about you. I want to let you know it's all going to work out," and you just became their miracle. Somebody is discouraged, saying, "God, I don't understand this subject. I'm not going to pass this course. God, send me somebody." You are that somebody.

Take time to become the miracle. Be aware of who is in your life. They're not there by accident. God put them there on purpose. It's because you are full of miracles.

> *There is healing in you. There is restoration, there's friendship, there are new beginnings.*

There is healing in you. There is restoration, there's friendship, there are new beginnings. Life is so much more rewarding when you realize you can be the answer to somebody's prayer. You can lift the fallen. You can restore the broken. You can be kind to a stranger. You can become someone's miracle.

A Miracle Waiting to Happen

My brother, Paul, is a surgeon. He spends a lot of time in Africa operating on needy people way back in the middle of nowhere. It's a remote village, hundreds of miles from the nearest city. The clinic is just a small tin building that barely has electricity, minimal medical supplies, and only one doctor. On a recent visit, a young man came into the clinic in the middle of the night who had been gored by an elephant tusk, right through his midsection. Paul took him back to the makeshift operating room to hopefully spare his life. The problem was that there was no blood in the blood supply with which to replenish the man. Paul could have thought, *Too bad. I'd love to help you, but you're going to need several pints of blood. It's just not your lucky day.* Before Paul operated, he took thirty minutes and gave his blood. He operated on the young man, then replenished the blood the man had lost with his own blood. What was he doing? Becoming a miracle. He could have prayed, "God, he's in bad shape. He needs a miracle." Paul realized, *I am his miracle.*

We all know that God can do great things. We know God can

do miracles. But what I want us to see is that He's put miracles in us. We can be the answer to someone's prayers. You can be the good break they're looking for. You can be the help they've been longing to have. It may not be something as dramatic as saving their life. It may be just teaching your coworker the skills you know. Or helping that family that's struggling with the rent. Or taking that young man to baseball practice with your son each week. It's no big deal to you, but it's a miracle to them. It's what will push them toward their destiny.

If we all had the attitude, *I am a miracle waiting to happen*, what kind of world would this be? I've heard it said, "Sometimes we don't need a miracle, we just need one another." Look around at who's in your life. Listen to what they're saying. Is there any way that you can help? Can you put in a good word for them at the office? Do they need a dress for a special occasion and you have a dozen in your closet you're never going to wear? Do they live alone and their family is in another state? You could invite them to have lunch with your family from time to time. Make them feel welcome. Those are opportunities to become their miracle.

"When You Refresh Others…"

A good friend of mine grew up very poor in the projects. He came from a single-parent family, and there wasn't always stability in the home. He loved to read and write, and his dream was to become a television journalist. Against all odds, he got a scholarship to a mostly white Ivy League university. He's African American. His roommate came from a very prestigious, influential family—just the opposite of his family. But these two young men hit it off and became the best of friends. He told his roommate about his desire to become a television journalist. His roommate said, "If you're going to be a journalist, you have to have a better vocabulary. You don't know enough words." Every day, this roommate would get the dictionary out and teach his friend one new word and have him use it in sentences all through the day. This went on for four straight years. What was this roommate doing? Becoming a miracle. He took the time to care. He realized his friend was in his life for a reason. Today, this young man is one of the top journalists in America. He works for a major network and is seen on one of the most prestigious news programs. But I wonder where he would be if his roommate had not taken the time to become a miracle.

"Well," you say, "I don't want to read about being a miracle. I need a miracle." Here's the key: If you will become a miracle, God will always make sure that you have the miracles that you need. As long as you're sowing these seeds, the right people, the right opportunities, and the breaks you need will be in your future. God will get you to where you're supposed to be. That's what it says in Proverbs: "When you refresh others, you will be refreshed." If you want your dream to come to pass, help somebody else's dream come to pass. If you need a miracle, become a miracle. When you take time to invest in others, the seeds you sow will always come back to you.

> *If you want your dream to come to pass, help somebody else's dream come to pass.*

I met two ladies after a service a few years ago, who I thought were mother and daughter. But the older lady said, "No, we're not, but she's just like my daughter." She told how before we moved our church from the northeast location of Houston to our new facility, she was very concerned about whether she would be able to continue to come. She's a widow and not comfortable driving the freeways. One day after a service, she was telling a group of friends her dilemma. This young lady, whom she had never met, overheard what she was saying, stepped up, and said, "How about I'll come pick you up each Sunday and bring you?" The lady was very surprised and looked at her and said, "Are you serious? Where do you live?" They lived thirty minutes apart. But that didn't stop this young lady. She could have thought, *I'd love to help you, but that's a long way, and I'm busy in my career and gas prices are really high.* Instead, she saw this as an opportunity to become a miracle. Now, every Sunday morning, like clockwork, she pulls up in the older lady's driveway at nine thirty in the morning and brings her to church. After the older lady told me the story, she hugged the young lady and said, "Joel, she's my miracle."

You can't help everyone, but you can help someone. There are people whom God has put in your path who are connected to your destiny. As you help them rise higher, you will rise higher. As you meet their needs, God will meet your needs. As you become a miracle, God will give you miracles. But just the opposite is true. If we're too busy to help someone else, we're not going to have the help we need. If we're too caught up in our own dreams to invest in others, or too worried about our own problems to encourage somebody else, we're going to get stuck. Reaching your highest potential is dependent on you helping someone else reach their potential. It's like a boomerang. When you help somebody else rise higher, it always comes back to you, and you'll rise higher.

You Are Full of Miracles

Jesus told a parable in Luke 10 about a man who was walking down a road when he was attacked and beaten by bandits. They left him on the ground, almost dead. In a little while, a priest came by. He saw the man from a distance and thought, *Boy, he's in bad shape. He sure needs a miracle. I'll be praying for him.* He kept on going. Then another man came by, a Levite, or an assistant to the priests, who did a little better. He went over to the man, checked him out, and felt sorry for him. He thought, *This is really unfair. I hope somebody helps him,* and went on down the road.

Then the third man, a Samaritan, came by. Like the first two, he thought, *He sure needs a miracle.* But he took it one step further and said, "You know what? I am his miracle. I'm at the right place at the right time. God put him in my path so I can be a healer, so I can be a restorer, so I can give him a new beginning." The Samaritan went to him, got down on his knees, and began to care for him. He gave him water from his canteen and took off his scarf and bandaged his wounds. The Samaritan then gently lifted him off the ground, placed him on his animal, and helped him mile after mile as they walked to the nearest city. When they got to the local inn, he pre-paid the owner and said, "You take care of him. Let him stay as long as he would like. Give him anything that he needs. And I promise that when I come back, I'll pay for any extra expenses."

My question is: Which man are you? It's easy to get so busy and think, *I don't have time to help others. I have my own problems.* Helping others can be the key to seeing your situation turn around. The people you see who need encouragement, who need a ride, who need blood, who need help accomplishing a dream—they are opportunities for you to go to a higher level. When you refresh others, you will be refreshed.

It's interesting that Jesus used a priest as an example in His par-able. He couldn't stop. He had to get to the temple. He had his reli-gious duties to fulfill. He didn't have time to bother with this man. After all, if he helped him, he might get his white robe bloody or "unclean." He might not look presentable at the temple. He had all kinds of excuses. But true religion gets dirty. True religion doesn't hide behind stained glass or fancy clothes. It goes to where the needs are.

> *True religion gets dirty. It goes to where the needs are.*

When you get down low to lift somebody up, in God's eyes, you can't get any higher. The closest thing to the heart of God is helping hurting people. When you take time to restore the broken, you pour the healing oil on their wounds, encouraging them, wiping away their tears, letting them know that there are new beginnings—that's the religion Jesus talked about. True religion doesn't judge people to see if they deserve our help. "Well, she's in need, but I don't think she's living the right kind of life." "He's hurting, but it's his own fault. He's got the addiction. He brought the trouble on himself."

Jesus said, "It's the sick who need the doctor, not the healthy." God didn't call us to judge people; He called us to heal people. He called us to restore people. He called us to become their miracles. Anybody can find fault. Anybody can be critical and come up with excuses to pass on by. That's easy. But where are the people who will take the time to care? Where are the people who will get down and dirty and help love them back into wholeness?

This third man, the Samaritan, immediately went to the man and started helping him, making a difference. He didn't think twice. He became the miracle. That's the kind of person I want us to be. Not passersby. Not too busy in our careers or with church work. Not people like the second man who feels sorry for them but says, "I wish it hadn't happened. I feel bad. I'm going to be praying." Let's become the miracle. God is counting on us. You can lift the fallen. You can heal the hurting. You can be a friend to the lonely. You can help a dream come to pass. You are full of miracles.

Pour Out the Healing Oil

Popular Christian singer Tammy Trent is a friend of mine. She told how she and her husband, Trent, went to a tropical island for a vacation to celebrate their eleventh wedding anniversary. Trent was a very skilled diver who could go underwater without an air tank for six or seven minutes at a time. They arrived at the beach on the first day so excited. Trent jumped in the water and started exploring the underwater caves. Tammy stayed on the beach to enjoy the beautiful scenery. Ten minutes went by, and she didn't see a sign of her husband, which made her a little worried. Twenty minutes, still no sign. Thirty minutes, and she still didn't see Trent. She began to panic and called the authorities. They sent out boats and started looking hour after hour. Unfortunately, they found Trent's lifeless body the next day.

Tammy was not only in shock and totally devastated, but she was in a foreign country, all alone, with nobody she knew. Her parents immediately made flight arrangements to come the next day. The problem is this all happened on September 10, 2001. The next day was 9/11. All flights were grounded. Tammy was there for days by herself, feeling alone and forgotten. She was so numb she couldn't even think straight. She finally was able to pray and said, "God, if You still care, send somebody to help me. God, send somebody to let me know that You are still there."

A few minutes later, there was a knock on her hotel door. It was the housekeeper, an older Jamaican woman. She said, "I don't mean to get in your business, but when I was cleaning the room next door, I couldn't help but hear you crying through the walls, and I was wondering if there is anything that I could pray with you about." Tammy told her what had happened, and the Jamaican housekeeper put her loving arms around Tammy and held her as though she was her own daughter. That moment, thousands of miles from home, Tammy knew that God was still in control. The housekeeper took the time to be a healer. She was sensitive to the needs around her, even hearing the cries from another room. She knew one reason she was here on Earth was to help wipe away the tears. That day she poured healing oil on Tammy's wounds. She became a miracle.

Show Them That You Care

The Scripture talks about how one day God will wipe away all the tears. There will be no tragedy, no more sickness, no more pain. But in the meantime, God is counting on you and me to wipe away those tears. Are you lifting the fallen? Are you restoring the broken? Are you taking time to help somebody in need? It's great to go to church and celebrate. This is important. We come to be encouraged and filled up and strengthened. But our real assignment begins when we leave the building. Look around and find the discouraged. Listen for the cries for help. You may not hear them with your ears, but you can hear them with your heart. You see when somebody is down. All of a sudden you feel that compassion flowing out to them. You think, *I need to take them out to dinner. I need to go encourage them.* Don't put it off. Don't be a passerby. That's God wanting you to bring healing. There's a tear that needs to be wiped away.

> *Are you lifting the fallen? Are you restoring the broken?*

Years ago I went into a restaurant to eat lunch. It was a little diner where you order your food up at the front. As I was walking to the counter, I saw this man sitting at a table by himself. When our eyes met, he nodded at me, and I immediately felt compassion toward him. I knew I was supposed to encourage him in some way. He was dressed in a nice suit and looked well-to-do. I was in my shorts and had our son, Jonathan, with me. He was about two years old at the time. I thought, *I'm not going to go encourage him. He's doing just fine.* I kept putting it off and putting it off.

I ordered our food, and on the way out, since the man had nodded at me, I decided to stop by his table. Just being friendly, I said, "Hello. How's it going?"

He kind of laughed and said, "Not very well. Things are kinda rough."

I didn't think much about it. I just smiled and said, "Well, I know this. It's going to get better."

He thanked me, and I left. That was the extent of the conversation.

A few months later, I received a letter in the mail from him. He told how he was at the lowest point of his life at that time. He was going through a divorce, and his whole world had fallen apart. For months he had been in depression. But he said, "When you made that statement that it's going to get better, it was like something reignited on the inside." That day was a turning point in his life. He came out of the depression. He got his fire back. Today, he is moving forward.

What I want you to see is that I didn't say anything profound. I didn't feel chill bumps when I said it. I simply took time to show him that I cared. We don't realize what we carry. We have the most powerful force in the universe inside us. What may seem ordinary to us, no big deal, becomes extraordinary when God breathes on it. It can be life-giving. A simple act of kindness.

> *We have the most powerful force in the universe inside us.*

A simple hug. Words of encouragement. Letting somebody know that you care. That can be the spark that brings them back to life.

Rescuing Hugs

In 1995, a young lady gave birth to twin girls. They were born very prematurely. One of the preemies was diagnosed with a severe heart problem and wasn't expected to live. The hospital's policy was to keep the babies in separate incubators. Several days passed, and the one baby continued to go downhill and was very close to death. One of the nurses felt strongly that the babies should be put in the same incubator as they had been in their mother's womb. After much hard work and much persuasion, she convinced the hospital to make an exception to their policy, and the babies were put in the same incubator side by side. Overnight, somehow the healthy baby managed to put her arm around her little sick sister. Much to everyone's surprise, the little sister's health started to improve. Her temperature came back to normal. Her heart stabilized. Little by little, day after day, she got better and better. Today, both of those young ladies are perfectly healthy. There is a very touching picture of the little baby with her arm around her sister; it's called "The Rescuing Hug."

We don't always see how powerful we really are. God has put healing in you. Your hugs can cause people to get better. Your kind words can put people back on their feet. The Scripture says, "A gentle tongue brings healing." A phone call, giving someone a ride, taking them out to dinner, encouraging them in their dreams—there are miracles in you waiting to happen. Some people just need to know that you believe in them. When you tell them, "You're amazing. You're going to do great things. I'm praying for you," it may seem simple to you, but to the other person it can be life-giving. It can help them blossom into all they were created to be.

> *"A gentle tongue brings healing."*

One time in the Scripture, Moses was on the top of this big hill watching a battle that was taking place. He was holding his rod up in the air. As long as he had his rod up, the Israelites were winning. But the battle went on hour after hour, and he got tired. Every time he put his hands down, the Amalekites would start to win. Finally, Moses couldn't take it any longer. He was too tired. His brother, Aaron, and a friend named Hur were with Moses on the mountain watching all this take place. They could have prayed, "God, we need a miracle. Keep the Amalekites from defeating us." Instead, they had this attitude: *We can become the miracle.* They got on each side of Moses, and they held his hands in the air. Because they became the miracle, the Israelites won the victory.

There are people God puts in our path who need us to hold up their hands. They're not going to win by themselves. They need your encouragement. They need your rescuing hug. They need to know that you care. They're praying for a miracle. Don't miss the opportunity. Do as Aaron and Hur did and become the miracle.

I saw a report on the news about a young lady named Meghan who was a junior in high school and a star long-distance runner on the track team. At the state track finals, she had already won first place in the sixteen-hundred-meter race. Next, she was competing in the thirty-two-hundred-meter race. As she came around the final curve, about fifty meters from the finish line, she saw the girl in front of her start to wobble, then her knees begin to buckle. The girl couldn't run in a straight line and she finally fell to the ground. What happened next made news around the world. Instead of Meghan passing her by, seeing that as an opportunity to beat another runner, Meghan stopped running, went over to the girl, picked her up off the ground, put her arm around her shoulders, and began to carry her toward the finish line.

The people in the stands began to cheer. There wasn't a dry eye in the place. When she got to the finish line, Meghan turned so her opponent could cross the line in front of her. Technically, they should have both been disqualified, because you're not allowed to touch another runner, but the state made an exception and gave them both a finishing time. Meghan said afterward, "Helping her cross that finish line was more satisfying to me than winning the state championship."

Your Light Will Break Forth

It's great to receive a miracle, but there's no greater feeling than to become a miracle. Who are you carrying? Who are you lifting up? Who are you helping to cross that finish line? Your destiny is connected to helping others.

Isaiah put it this way: "When you feed the hungry, when you clothe the naked, when you help those in need, then your light will break forth like the dawn and your healing will quickly come." If you will make it your business to become a miracle, God will make it His business to give you miracles. You will never lack His blessings and favor.

Friend, you are the answer to somebody's prayer. You can give a rescuing hug this week. You can help a friend cross the finish line. You are the miracle that they're believing for. When you go out each day, have this attitude: *I am a miracle waiting to happen.* If you will live not thinking about how you can get a miracle, but how you can become a miracle, then just as God promised, your light is going to break forth like the dawn. Your healing, your promotion, and your vindication will quickly come.

We Want to Hear from You!

Each week, I close our international television broadcast by giving the audience an opportunity to make Jesus the Lord of their lives. I'd like to extend that same opportunity to you.

Are you at peace with God? A void exists in every person's heart that only God can fill. I'm not talking about joining a church or finding religion. I'm talking about finding life and peace and happiness. Would you pray with me today? Just say, "Lord Jesus, I repent of my sins. I ask You to come into my heart. I make You my Lord and Savior."

Friend, if you prayed that simple prayer, I believe you have been "born again." I encourage you to attend a good, Bible-based church and keep God in first place in your life. For free information on how you can grow stronger in your spiritual life, please feel free to contact us.

Victoria and I love you, and we'll be praying for you. We're believing for God's best for you, that you will see your dreams come to pass. We'd love to hear from you!

To contact us, write to:

Joel and Victoria Osteen
P.O. Box 4600
Houston, TX 77210

Or you can reach us online at www.joelosteen.com.